AF469335

NOTTINGHAMSHIRE CCC
On This Day

NOTTINGHAMSHIRE CCC
On This Day

*History, Facts & Figures
from Every Day of the Year*

DAVE BRACEGIRDLE

NOTTINGHAMSHIRE CCC
On This Day

History, Facts & Figures
from Every Day of the Year

All statistics, facts and figures are correct as of 31st January 2012

© Dave Bracegirdle

Dave Bracegirdle has asserted his rights in accordance with the Copyright, Designs and Patents Act 1988 to be identified as the author of this work.

Published By:
Pitch Publishing (Brighton) Ltd
A2 Yeoman Gate
Yeoman Way
Durrington
BN13 3QZ

Email: info@pitchpublishing.co.uk
Web: www.pitchpublishing.co.uk

First published 2012

A catalogue record for this book is available from the British Library.

ISBN 978-1-9080515-8-5
Typesetting and origination by Pitch Publishing. Printed in Great Britain.
Manufacturing managed by Jellyfish Print Solutions Ltd.

FOREWORD BY PETER WRIGHT

Nottinghamshire County Cricket Club is at the very forefront of our summer game and I'm delighted and honoured that I've been involved during the last two decades in formulating the development strategy of this great club and witnessed at close quarters the hard work that has been put in to ensure that Trent Bridge and the team on the field remain at the pinnacle of our game.

The awarding of two Ashes Test matches, to be played in Nottingham in 2013 and 2015, and an Indian Test in 2014 is deserved recognition for our long-term plan to provide the very best, both in playing facilities and spectator comfort, and we will endeavour to ensure that those standards are continually reviewed and improved upon, to ensure we retain our status as one of the finest and friendliest cricket grounds in the world.

In recent years we have seen some wonderful new developments at Trent Bridge, new stands, the installation of our permanent floodlight pylons, a re-laid outfield, a spectacular video screen and an excellent administrative centre.

Having such a wonderful arena wouldn't count for much if similar attention hadn't been paid to keeping the team competitive. From our respected academy set-up, through the various age groups and on into the first-team, our cricketers are coached to the highest-possible standards as we strive to challenge for honours, whilst also playing the game in the spirit it was intended.

By its very nature, we get so much enjoyment from our sport and I can't fully begin to equate how important a role cricket has played in my life.

From the moment I first visited Trent Bridge, as a seven-year-old with my elder brother, I fell in love with the place. Running the old scoreboard, next to the old ladies' pavilion, with my brother a few years later taught me to concentrate on the game and particularly the way different players approached it. I believe cricket engenders great team spirit and mutual respect that can influence people's lives for the better.

As we approach the 175th anniversary of cricket at Trent Bridge it is perhaps poignant not only to look to the exciting times ahead but also to cast a glance in the rear-view mirror at some of those personalities that have played such a prominent role in our story.

From William Clarke, the great visionary, who helped create the ground we play on today, to the 19th-century players who were involved at the birth of the county game and then the beginning of Test match cricket, through the era of Larwood and Voce – names that have become synonymous with some of the toughest and most combative periods in the game – and on into the modern era.

Nottinghamshire County Cricket Club set the bar high with the signing of Garfield Sobers in 1968 and since then a succession of overseas stars have been welcomed into our city and into our hearts and many have been involved in some of our biggest successes.

Their individual skills and experience has rubbed off on some of our home-grown talent and, together with our own excellent coaching staff, has helped us maintain our station as a regular supplier of talent for the international arena.

Those that are privileged to wear the county colours nowadays do so with our best wishes and join a long list of players that have been associated with the club.

All have their own story to tell and many are featured inside the cover of this book, which has been lovingly researched by the author, with attention paid to not only the most significant milestones but also the quirky, easily forgotten moments.

I have thoroughly enjoyed reading *Nottinghamshire CCC On This Day* and hope you will as well.

Peter Wright, Chairman Nottinghamshire CCC

ACKNOWLEDGEMENTS

Without the help of a significant number of people this book wouldn't have seen the light of day and many of them aren't around to be thanked personally. As you'll discover, some of the many key personalities that have helped shape Nottinghamshire's future were involved in the very early stages of the club's existence.

That we know so much about them and their performances is due to the diligent recording of facts and figures by the early scorers and historians. Their successors have continued to tell the county's story in print, making the task of putting this work together much easier that it would have been otherwise.

Thanks need to be passed to the various contributors to the *Wisden Cricketers' Almanak*, the Notts CCC annuals, plus assorted cricket magazines, internet sites, books, brochures and scorecards. My own collection has helped with the task of tracking down and confirming some of the facts but when I've run dry of information or needed clarification I've known where to turn to.

The help of Peter Wynne-Thomas has been invaluable in either settling my curiosity or steering me towards an answer.

So many other people, perhaps unknowingly, have been a source of information and deserve acknowledgement. Thanks then, to Michael Temple, Chris Botherway and Tom Paterson for their assistance and tolerance of my frequent queries, to Derek Brewer and Lisa Pursehouse for their support, to Paul Johnson and Mick Newell for filling in some of the blanks and to John Ellison, a valued friend.

The photographs in this book have kindly been supplied by nottsccc.co.uk, the Portrait Collective and the *Nottingham Post*, with yours truly on hand to capture the moment when Chris Read and the team celebrated their Emirates Airline Twenty20 success in Dubai.

Thanks also, to Paul and Jane Camillin, at Pitch Publishing, for their expertise and for presenting me with the opportunity of putting this work together and to Peter Wright, chairman of the club, who has overseen so many developments at Trent Bridge and has kindly contributed the foreword.

INTRODUCTION

There wasn't too much to enthuse over when the Nottinghamshire team visited Hove in May 2011. Having watched them lose to Sussex inside three days, I then sat with the players as we collectively watched Nottingham Forest miss out on a trip to Wembley for the Championship play-off final.

Indeed, the only upside to the week came when I met Pitch Publishing's Paul Camillin and he asked me to put together this book, chronicling the history, the major events and players of my favourite county side, in diary form.

"That won't take long," I misguidedly thought. As it turned out, it was a good job that the publishers gave me a deadline date because a project such as this can be never-ending.

There is an old saying "the more you look, the more you see" and never was it better illustrated than by several months scouring through playing records and scorecards. I'm sure this book doesn't offer a comprehensive collection of 'every' key moment in the Nottinghamshire story.

Hopefully the major ones are all covered and the leading performers all get a mention – one way or another. I'm only too aware though that many important personalities aren't included – club officials, groundstaff (and the club has had some of the very best in the history of the game) and many players.

To them, my apologies, but surely there are still enough stats, trivia and information to satisfy even the most casual of supporters and in line with the brief, there's an incident, moment, match, birth or death for every day of the year (thank heavens for winter tours!).

Invariably a book of this type becomes outdated almost as soon as it has been published. I would like to think that a follow-up copy in two or three years' time would be able to include details of another County Championship success, a Lord's final and a much-treasured first domestic Twenty20 success, as well as the next batch of players who have made the step up from the county game into the international arena.

I have gleaned so much pleasure from watching Nottinghamshire play over the years – particularly at Trent Bridge (there is no finer cricket ground) – and I've probably gained just as much satisfaction from writing about the important milestones and characters that have helped shape the county's fortunes.

Whether this book enriches your knowledge or brings back some very fond memories I hope you enjoy reading *Nottinghamshire CCC On This Day*.

Dave Bracegirdle

NOTTINGHAMSHIRE CCC
On This Day

JANUARY

SATURDAY 1st JANUARY 1977

Derek Randall made his England Test debut against India at Eden Gardens, Calcutta. Although the tourists had convincingly won the first of the five-match series they made a couple of changes for the New Years Day fixture, with Randall and Leicestershire's Roger Tolchard each being selected for their first international appearance. The Nottinghamshire man made 37 but was only required to bat once as England completed a ten-wicket victory.

THURSDAY 1st JANUARY 1987

Nottinghamshire's opening batsman Chris Broad played in 34 one-day internationals for England, starting with a fixture against Australia at the WACA in Perth. Broad top scored with 76 out of a total of 272-6 but the man of the match award went to Ian Botham for a typically robust 68 which came from just 39 balls faced. The match was England's first in the Benson and Hedges Challenge, a four-team tournament which also featured Pakistan and the West Indies. England won all three of their group matches, before triumphing over Pakistan in the final.

MONDAY 1st JANUARY 1990

A veteran of 23 Test matches for England, Joseph Hardstaff junior died in a Worksop hospital, aged 78. Following in the footsteps of his father, Joseph Hardstaff senior, he entered county cricket with Nottinghamshire at the age of 19 and scored 53 not out in his debut innings. In a prolific career, which stretched from 1930-1955, although interrupted throughout the war, the right-handed top-order batsman scored over 24,000 runs for Notts, including 65 centuries. He also scored five international hundreds, with a best of 205 not out, scored against India at Lord's in 1946.

SATURDAY 2nd JANUARY 1904

George Frank Henry Heane was born in Worksop and made 172 appearances for Nottinghamshire between 1927 and 1951. A left-handed batsman, he scored 5,854 runs for the county at an average of 26.97, with nine centuries and a personal best of 138. His right-arm medium-paced bowling produced 201 wickets, with a best of 6-52. Heane captained Notts between 1935 and 1946 and died in Lincolnshire in 1969.

WEDNESDAY 3rd JANUARY 1951

Reg Simpson scored 64 centuries during his first-class career, 48 coming for Nottinghamshire. His highest innings came on tour with MCC in Australia. Playing against New South Wales at the SCG, he shared in stands of 236 with Len Hutton (150) and 228 with Gilbert Parkhouse (92). Having passed his previous career-best score of 243, Simpson went on to make 259 before losing his wicket to the off-break bowler, Jim Burke. Despite MCC extending their innings to 553-8 declared they weren't able to bowl out the home side for a second time as the contest ended in a draw.

TUESDAY 3rd JANUARY 1989

Alexander Daniel Hales was born in Hillingdon, Middlesex and sprang to prominence as an MCC Young Cricketer. After successfully trialing with Nottinghamshire, the right-handed batsman signed his first professional contract in 2007 and made his List A and first-class debuts the following year. His 150 against Worcestershire was the highest Pro40 score of 2009 and his maiden championship hundred came a year later against Hampshire. In 2011, after scoring 184 at Trent Bridge against Somerset, he was awarded his county cap and subsequently earned selection for the England Lions, before making his full international debut in a Twenty20 fixture against India.

FRIDAY 4th JANUARY 1991

Eddie Hemmings played 16 Tests for England between 1982 and his final one, which was against Australia at the Sydney Cricket Ground. In a drawn fixture, the off-spinner couldn't complain of being under-used. In the first innings he bowled 32 overs and took 3-105, whilst second time around he took 3-94 from 41 overs. The Nottinghamshire man claimed a total of 43 Test wickets, with a best of 6-58.

WEDNESDAY 5th JANUARY 1972

Garfield Sobers scored 254, whilst captaining a Rest of the World XI at the Melbourne Cricket Ground, in a five-day unofficial Test match against Australia. The Nottinghamshire and West Indies left-hander batted for 376 minutes and hit 33 fours and two sixes. A watching Don Bradman described the performance as: "Probably the greatest exhibition of batting ever seen in Australia."

FRIDAY 6th JANUARY 1978

Charles Edward "Charlie" Shreck was born in Truro, Cornwall, and served his apprenticeship playing for his home county in the Minor Counties championship. He made his first-class debut for Nottinghamshire in 2003 and went on to take 293 wickets in 83 matches. At 6'7" tall, Shreck was a formidable new-ball bowler and took five wickets in an innings on 15 occasions for the county. His best figures for Notts were 8-31 against Middlesex at Trent Bridge in 2006. A member of the County Championship-winning squad in 2010, Shreck signed for Kent at the end of the following season.

SUNDAY 7th JANUARY 1838

The younger brother of the better-known George and Samuel Parr, who both played for Nottinghamshire, Henry John Parr was born in Radcliffe-on-Trent. As a lower-order batsman, he made just 55 runs from his three appearances for the county, with a best score of 13 at The Oval against Surrey in 1858. Henry Parr also played in some matches for the All England Eleven but his life was cut short when he died aged 25.

TUESDAY 7th JANUARY 1947

After a wonderful career, Nottinghamshire's Bill Voce bowed out of Test cricket on a rather subdued note. Playing against Australia at the MCG in the third match of the series he failed to take a wicket in his 27th and final Test and was then dismissed first ball by Bruce Dooland, who joined the Trent Bridge staff six years later. Voce took 98 wickets for England at 27.88, with his left-arm fast-medium bowling, with a best of 7-71.

FRIDAY 7th JANUARY 1983

Having gone to the wicket as a night-watchman for England in the final Test of the series against Australia at the Sydney Cricket Ground, Nottinghamshire's Eddie Hemmings batted for much of the final day to help secure a draw but was then cruelly dismissed when just five runs short of a century. His 95 comfortably beat his previous highest score for his country – the 29 he had scored in the first innings of the same match!

SUNDAY 8th JANUARY 2006

Chris Cairns played in 96 List A matches for Nottinghamshire, taking 135 wickets and scoring 2,677 runs at an average of 41.82. He also played in 214 one-day internationals for New Zealand, playing the final one on this day against Sri Lanka in Napier. The all-rounder scored 4,881 runs for his country at this level and took exactly 200 wickets.

TUESDAY 9th JANUARY 1968

James Clive "Jimmy" Adams was born in Port Maria, St Mary, Jamaica. The left-handed batsman and slow left-arm bowler went on to play in 54 Test matches for the West Indies, captaining them on 15 occasions between 2000 and 2001. In 1994, Adams had played in 18 first-class matches for Nottinghamshire, scoring 950 runs, with three centuries, at an average of 35.18 and taking 23 wickets at 31.3. He scored a further 819 runs at 51.18 from his 20 List A matches for the county and took a further six wickets.

FRIDAY 10th JANUARY 1936

Charles William Wright was 72 when he died at Saxelby Park, near to Melton Mowbray. As a right-handed batsman and wicketkeeper he made three Test appearances for England and went on four overseas tours, two to the USA and Canada, one to India and one to South Africa where he made his international appearances in 1896. For Nottinghamshire, Wright played in 117 matches, scoring 2,565 runs, with a best of 99. He was forced to retire from the game after losing an eye in a shooting accident and later became a long-standing member of the Nottinghamshire Cricket Club's committee.

WEDNESDAY 10th JANUARY 1979

It was a case of the end justifying the means as Derek Randall ground out the slowest century in matches between England and Australia, in terms of balls received. His hundred came up in 406 minutes, from 353 deliveries, but the Nottinghamshire man went on to eventually reach 150 at the Sydney Cricket Ground, an innings that broke the resistance of the home side and set England up to achieve an Ashes-securing victory the following day.

SATURDAY 11th JANUARY 1930

Twenty-two of the 27 Tests played by Bill Voce were overseas, beginning with his debut against the West Indies in Bridgetown. Nottinghamshire's left-arm fast-medium bowler took 2-120 on his first appearance for England.

FRIDAY 12th JANUARY 1945

Harry Butler Daft was 78 when he died in High Cross, Hertfordshire. A multi-talented sportsman, he made five appearances for the England football team, scoring three times. Most of his club football was played for Notts County, where he won the FA Cup in 1894. He was also an outstanding servant to Nottinghamshire County Cricket Club. Between 1885 and 1899 he made 200 appearances, scoring 4,370 runs, with a best of 92, and taking 86 wickets with the ball. Harry's father, Richard Daft, had been an outstanding batsman for the county and in August 1891, in a fixture against Surrey at The Oval, he returned to help a side handicapped by injury, to appear in the county XI with his son for the only time.

FRIDAY 13th JANUARY 1933

The Adelaide Oval, home of the third Test between Australia and England, was the ground where the Bodyline controversy was at its worst. Nottinghamshire's Harold Larwood bore the full brunt of the crowd's dissatisfaction as he struck two home batsmen. Bill Woodfull received a nasty blow above the heart and Bert Oldfield had to retire hurt with a fractured skull when attempting a hook, although he later refused to blame the bowler for his injury. With a strong leg-side field, set by England captain Douglas Jardine, relations between the two sides became extremely heated.

FRIDAY 14th JANUARY 1887

England's tour of Australia was run by former Nottinghamshire player Alf Shaw and in the non-Test fixtures the side even played under the name A Shaw's XI. Six members of the touring party were from Notts and five played in a match at Bathurst. Wilf Flowers was unavailable for selection but Arthur Shrewsbury, William Scotton, Mordecai Sherwin, George Gunn and Billy Barnes were involved as the match was drawn.

WEDNESDAY 15th JANUARY 1947

Graham Frost was born in Old Basford and played in 102 first-class matches for Notts between 1967 and 1973. He amassed 3,439 runs at 22.62, with a best of 107 versus Surrey in 1970. Although he took only 15 wickets in the longer format, he collected 40 more from just 68 List A matches with a best of 5-33 against Worcestershire at Newark in 1971.

SUNDAY 15th JANUARY 1978

Born in Huddersfield, Yorkshire, Ryan Jay Sidebottom spent seven years with Nottinghamshire, sandwiched between two spells for the county of his birth. A left-arm quick bowler, he played in 65 first-class matches for Notts, taking 216 wickets at 25.20. Forty-seven List A matches produced 43 wickets and a further 25 wickets came in 25 Twenty20 contests. A member of the side which won the County Championship in 2005 and 2010, Sidebottom was also an England regular in all three formats of the game during his time with the county. His father Arnold had made one Test appearance for England, against Australia at Trent Bridge in 1985.

WEDNESDAY 16th JANUARY 1907

The man who bowled the first ball in Test cricket died at Gedling, Nottinghamshire, aged 64. Alf Shaw was a right-arm medium-pace bowler who made his Notts debut in 1864 and went on to take 898 wickets in 193 matches, ranking him 11th on Nottinghamshire's all-time list of wicket-takers. Shaw played seven times for England, six of the matches in Australia, where he played in the opening fixture in 1877 and went on to organise later tours there himself.

SUNDAY 16th JANUARY 1925

The Test debut of William Wilfred "Dodger" Whysall came in the third match of England's tour of Australia at the Adelaide Oval. The Nottinghamshire opener scored just nine in his first knock for his country but fared better in the second innings, scoring 75 – although he had been lowered to number five in the batting order. This was the third successive match that went into a seventh day but eventually, like the previous two, it was won by Australia.

MONDAY 17th JANUARY 1916

Left-handed batsman and slow left-arm spinner Frederick Henry "Harry" Winrow was born in Manton, Nottinghamshire. He made his debut at Lord's against Middlesex in 1938 and played 113 first-class matches for Notts. He was awarded his county cap in 1947, the same year in which he recorded the best score of his career, 204 not out against Derbyshire at Trent Bridge.

THURSDAY 18th JANUARY 1866

Born in Radford, William Naylor Kirk made just one appearance for Nottinghamshire. He played against MCC at Lord's in 1888, making just four runs in his only innings. Kirk later played Minor Counties cricket for Herefordshire and died in Hyson Green just short of his 38th birthday.

TUESDAY 19th JANUARY 1999

Chris Cairns played many destructive innings for Nottinghamshire during his lengthy on-off association with them, which stretched from 1988 until 2006, although few could match his ODI knock for New Zealand against India in Christchurch. With the series up for grabs, Cairns scored a brutal century from just 75 deliveries, eventually ending on 115 off 80 balls, with seven boundaries and seven sixes.

WEDNESDAY 20th JANUARY 1864

Nottinghamshire captain George Parr took a touring side to Australia, including county team-mate Cris Tinley. Against Maryborough, a side from Queensland, the tourists agreed for the opposition to play with 22 men. Despite this numerical disadvantage Parr's XI still won by an innings, with Tinley, an underarm right-arm slow bowler, taking 11-24 in the first innings and 11-48 in the second!

SATURDAY 21st JANUARY 1928

Samuel Staples, elder brother of Arthur Staples – who also enjoyed a lengthy career with Nottinghamshire – made the first of his three England appearances against South Africa in Durban. An accurate medium-paced bowler, he claimed five wickets in the match, the third in the series. He took a further ten wickets in the final two Tests, to give him a three-match haul of 15-435 but he was then surprisingly overlooked and didn't play for his country again.

Nottinghamshire County Eleven, 1929.

WINNERS OF THE COUNTY CHAMPIONSHIP

Matches played 28   Won 14   Lost 2   Won 1st inns. 4   Lost 1st inns. 6   No result 2   Points 158

Standing :.
LARWOOD, H.   STAPLES, S. J.   VOCE, W.   WHYSALL, W. W.   WALKER, W.   PAYTON, W.

Seated :..
LILLEY, B.   STAPLES, A.   A. W. CARR, (CAPTAIN).   GUNN, G.   BARRATT, F.

SUNDAY 22nd JANUARY 1815

Charles Brown made 23 first-class appearances for Nottinghamshire in a career from 1843 to 1861. A right-handed batsman, his top score for the county was only 36 but his main attribute was his wicketkeeping, particularly standing up, where he claimed 22 stumpings out of the 46 dismissals he was involved in. Brown only ever played a handful of games each season but was last called upon aged 46. He died in Nottingham, the city of his birth, in 1875.

SUNDAY 23rd JANUARY 2000

Chris Read played in 36 one-day internationals for England between 2000 and 2006. His debut came against South Africa in Bloemfontein. The Notts wicketkeeper caught Gary Kirsten and Hansie Cronje as the home side were dismissed for just 184. England then cantered to a nine-wicket success, thanks to 85 from captain Nasser Hussain and an unbeaten 71 from Nick Knight. Apart from it being Read's first match, there was also a debut for Northants spinner Graeme Swann – his sole ODI for seven years, by which time he'd become a Nottinghamshire player.

FRIDAY 24th JANUARY 1947

Bill Taylor was an attacking new-ball bowler, who took 211 wickets for Notts in 95 matches between 1971 and 1977. Manchester-born, his best figures were 6-42, against Warwickshire in 1972. He also played in 122 List A matches, which reaped 170 wickets at 24.08. Whilst his batting didn't often make the headlines, he came to Nottinghamshire's rescue in a 1975 Gillette Cup first round tie at home to Sussex. Number 11 on the card, he blasted 63 from 31 balls to power his side to an unexpected victory and collect a deserved man of the match award for scoring the only 50 of his county career.

SATURDAY 25th JANUARY 1930

Born in Nottingham, Alan Kenneth Armitage only played five matches for his home county, scoring 160 runs, with a best of 43 not out against Somerset in 1951. A right-handed batsman and occasional wicketkeeper, he registered one first-class century though, batting for Oxford University against Free Foresters at The Parks.

WEDNESDAY 26th JANUARY 1983

In just his third one-day international for England – and first overseas – Eddie Hemmings took 3-11 at the SCG as England defeated Australia by 98 runs. Derek Randall, his county colleague, top-scored for the tourists with 47.

MONDAY 27th JANUARY 1964

Christopher Wilmot Scott was born at Thorpe-on-the-Hill, Lincolnshire. Between 1981 and 1991 the wicketkeeper played 63 first-class matches for Nottinghamshire, claiming 144 dismissals (135 catches and nine stumpings), as well as scoring 1,263 runs, with a best of 78. Scott also played in 32 List A matches for Notts, before leaving to join Durham in 1992.

SATURDAY 27th JANUARY 1979

Born in Auckland, New Zealand, Daniel Luca Vettori became the youngest player to represent his country when he made his Test debut aged 18 in 1997. Six years later, the slow left-arm spinner spent a brief period with Notts, playing two first-class matches, against India A and Kent, and one National League 45-over game at The Rose Bowl against Hampshire.

TUESDAY 28th JANUARY 1947

Born on this day, Peter John Plummer took 63 first-class wickets in 33 matches for Nottinghamshire between 1969 and 1972. The left-arm spinner's best performance came against Oxford University in 1972, when he took 7-71. He also played in 12 List A matches, where his best performance came on debut, 5-44 against Yorkshire at Bradford.

WEDNESDAY 29th JANUARY 1947

Former England fast bowler Fred Barratt was 52 when he died in Nottingham General Hospital. The Nottinghamshire quickie had burst onto the county scene in 1914, taking eight wickets on debut. He went on to make five Test appearances and played in a total of 353 matches for Notts, taking 1,176 wickets at 22.36 each. Towards the end of his career he was being labelled as a true all-rounder, achieving the double of 1,000 runs and 100 wickets in 1928 and following it up with his most prolific season with the ball, collecting 129 wickets in the 1929 County Championship triumph.

SATURDAY 30th JANUARY 1988

Chris Broad found himself in hot water after a display of petulance. The Nottinghamshire opener showed his frustration at getting out by knocking over his leg stump with his bat as he departed. Fined £500 by the tour management for his indiscretion, the left-hander at least had the satisfaction of having scored 139 before the incident happened. Broad was playing for England at the time, against Australia in a one-off Test match in Sydney to celebrate their bicentenary of permanent white settlement. County colleagues Tim Robinson, Bruce French and Eddie Hemmings also took part in the match, which ended in a draw.

MONDAY 31st JANUARY 1887

Nottinghamshire's Billy Barnes compiled his best Test match figures of 6-28 to help England defeat Australia at Sydney. Apart from Barnes, five of his county team-mates were also in the visiting side, including debutants William Gunn and Mordecai Sherwin. Astonishingly, the match had begun with England being dismissed for just 45 in their first innings.

WEDNESDAY 31st JANUARY 1934

John "Brian" Bolus joined Notts from his native Yorkshire in 1963 and within two months of his debut was back at Headingley, preparing to face the West Indies on his England Test debut. A reliable accumulator of runs, Bolus scored 15,493 in 269 first-class matches whilst with Nottinghamshire, averaging 35.29. The largest of his 25 centuries came against Glamorgan at Trent Bridge, when he scored 202 not out in his first season with the county. Born close to Leeds, he had made more than 100 appearances for his first county and later spent three seasons with Derbyshire.

NOTTINGHAMSHIRE CCC
On This Day

FEBRUARY

MONDAY 1st FEBRUARY 1965

David John Callaghan was born in Queenstown, Cape Province, South Africa. Although predominantly known as a hard hitting, right-handed batsman he was a useful medium-pace bowler and in this capacity he left his mark in the Nottinghamshire record books. In his only first-class fixture for an English county, against the touring West Indians, Callaghan clean bowled Keith Arthurton, becoming only the fourth player to take a wicket with his first delivery for the county.

SUNDAY 1st FEBRUARY 1998

Nottinghamshire's young all-rounder Paul Franks became a World Cup winner with the England Under-19 side that defeated New Zealand in the final at the New Wanderers Stadium in Johannesburg. Franks took 1-49 with the ball and made 16 as England successfully chased down 242 to win by seven wickets. Graeme Swann and Richard Logan, both players to join Notts later in their careers, were also in the winning side.

THURSDAY 2nd FEBRUARY 1933

Harold Larwood's best bowling performance in Australia came in a non first-class match on the 1932-33 winter tour. Playing in a two-day fixture against Queensland Country at the Showground at Toowomba, the Nottinghamshire fast bowler took 8-28, with seven of his victims all being clean bowled.

FRIDAY 2nd FEBRUARY 1973

Richard Hadlee made his Test debut, playing for New Zealand against Pakistan in Wellington. The all-rounder, who represented Nottinghamshire between 1978 and 1987, took 2-84 in the first innings, with former Kent batsman Asif Iqbal his first victim. Hadlee scored 46 then failed to take a wicket in Pakistan's second innings as the match petered out into a draw.

SUNDAY 2nd FEBRUARY 1975

At the Barbados Garrison Racecourse, barely a mile from where he was born in Walcott Avenue, Garfield Sobers was knighted by Her Majesty Queen Elizabeth II for his services to cricket. The award was originally intended to be made in the 1975 Queen's Birthday Honours but was moved forward to coincide with her visit to Barbados.

SATURDAY 3rd FEBRUARY 1979

Paul John Franks was born in Mansfield and made his Nottinghamshire debut in a championship match against Hampshire in 1996. Over the next 14 seasons the all-rounder scored more than 6,000 runs and claimed almost 500 wickets in first-class fixtures. But for an unfortunate run of injuries he would surely have played for his country on more occasions than the sole appearance which came at Trent Bridge, his home ground, against the West Indies in 2000.

SATURDAY 4th FEBRUARY 1899

Arthur Staples played for Nottinghamshire between 1924 and 1938, scoring 12,762 runs and taking 635 wickets in 358 matches. He made an immediate impact, becoming only the third Notts player to take a wicket with his opening delivery in first-class cricket, that of Worcestershire's Ronald Holyoake. Born at Newstead Colliery, he was a fine right-handed batsman and registered 12 centuries. During the off-season he played in goal for both Mansfield Town and Bournemouth. Staples, the younger brother of Test player Sam Staples, died in 1965, aged 66.

THURSDAY 4th FEBRUARY 1971

Born in Nottingham, Wayne Anthony Dessaur made his first-class debut for his home county in 1992, dismissed by Northamptonshire's West Indian fast bowler Curtly Ambrose for just one in his first championship innings. The right-handed batsman recovered from that early setback to score a century in his next outing, making a career-best 148 at Trent Bridge, against Cambridge University. Dessaur scored 643 runs for Notts, averaging just over 30, but after just 16 matches he was allowed to move to Derbyshire, where he scored a century on debut.

FRIDAY 5th FEBRUARY 1971

Wayne Michael Noon was born in Grimsby, Lincolnshire, and joined the Trent Bridge staff in 1994 after beginning his first-class career with Northamptonshire. The wicketkeeper claimed 193 victims for Nottinghamshire in just 78 appearances, including a county-best seven catches in an innings against Kent in 1991. A further 85 dismissals came from 92 List A fixtures. Noon also scored 2,340 runs for Notts, with a best of 83, before joining the county's coaching staff.

SUNDAY 5th FEBRUARY 1984

Nottinghamshire's Richard Hadlee turned in a sensational performance to inflict England's heaviest Test defeat for 11 years. At Christchurch, the New Zealander scored 99 from just 81 deliveries, in only 111 minutes. He then took 3-16, including the wicket of county team-mate Derek Randall for a duck, plus 5-28 in England's follow-on. The margin of victory was an innings and 132 runs.

MONDAY 6th FEBRUARY 1989

Darren Michael Bravo was born in Santa Cruz, Trinidad, and played Test, one-day and Twenty20 international cricket for the West Indies before joining Nottinghamshire on a short-term contract at the end of the 2011 season. Aged just 22, the left-handed batsman scored 248 runs in four first-class matches at an average of 35.42 and 94 runs from three List A appearances.

THURSDAY 6th FEBRUARY 1930

Nottinghamshire's Bill Voce represented England in 27 Tests but the left-arm pace bowler's best figures came in just his second international appearance, taking 7-70 against the West Indies in Trinidad as England went one up in the series.

THURSDAY 7th FEBRUARY 1963

Captain of Nottinghamshire between 1919 and 1934, Arthur Carr died at West Witton in Yorkshire. He scored 18,885 runs for the county in 416 matches, which included 43 centuries and a top score of 206 not out. His best form deserted him on international duty though, with his 63 against South Africa at Johannesburg in 1922 the only time he passed 50 in 11 Test appearances.

MONDAY 8th FEBRUARY 1909

William Arnold Sime was born in Orange Free State, South Africa, and played for the Minor Counties and Oxford University before joining Nottinghamshire in 1925. A right-handed batsman, he scored 2,328 runs at an average of 19.89 and took 44 wickets at 47.5 with his slow left-arm bowling. Despite those relatively modest figures he made 91 appearances for Notts and remained with them for 25 years, captaining the side between 1947 and 1950.

SUNDAY 9th FEBRUARY 2003

Paul Franks scored 41 in a second-innings knock for Canterbury at Auckland in New Zealand's State Championship. Despite bowling 38 overs in the match, the Nottinghamshire all-rounder failed to pick up a wicket in his only first-class appearance for the side and also finished on the losing team.

WEDNESDAY 10th FEBRUARY 1965

Cecil Alfred Leonard Sutton was 79 when he passed away in Whatton, Nottinghamshire. A right-handed batsman and right-arm medium-pace bowler, he made just one appearance for Notts. Playing against MCC at Lord's in 1907, he scored a single from his only innings and failed to take a wicket from the seven overs he sent down.

WEDNESDAY 11th FEBRUARY 1970

Alistair Duncan Brown was born at Beckenham, Kent, but spent 17 seasons with Surrey before joining Notts in 2009. After arriving at Trent Bridge, the former England ODI batsman became a virtual ever-present in all three formats of the game, helping the side to County Championship success in 2010, as well as an appearance at Twenty20 Finals Day the same summer. Brown retired from the playing side in 2011 and was announced as the new second XI coach at Surrey shortly afterwards.

FRIDAY 11th FEBRUARY 2011

Nottinghamshire cricket mourned the loss of John Desmond Clay, who died at the age of 86. A right-handed batsman, he played in 236 first-class games for Notts between 1948 and 1961, captaining the side in his final year. He scored a total of 9,991 runs at an average of 26.08, with 11 centuries and a top score of 192.

MONDAY 12th FEBRUARY 1940

Born in Bolsover, Derbyshire, Joseph Walters was a leg-break bowler who played five first-class matches for Nottinghamshire in the late 1950s, taking just ten wickets. His best performance for the county came in a two-day friendly against the Royal Air Force at Trent Bridge. He backed up first-innings figures of 8-59 with 5-49, claiming future England captain AR (Tony) Lewis amongst his victims.

MONDAY 13th FEBRUARY 1882

Born in Stapleford, Notts, Wilfred Richard Daniel Payton scored 39 centuries for his home county in 489 matches. His 22,079 runs, scored between 1905 and 1931, puts him eighth on the list of Nottinghamshire's highest run-scorers in first-class cricket. Wilf's brother, Albert (one match), and son, also Wilfred (27 matches), both represented the county as well.

WEDNESDAY 13th FEBRUARY 1991

Chris Cairns had already spent two seasons on the Trent Bridge staff before his maiden ODI for New Zealand. The Kiwi all-rounder made a total of 215 appearances at this level for his country with the first coming at Wellington against the touring England side. Cairns scored five out of a total of 196-8 but then collected figures of 2-41 with the ball, taking the wickets of Graham Gooch and Allan Lamb, in his side's nine-run victory.

MONDAY 14th FEBRUARY 1944

Joe Hardstaff junior was one of the many first-class cricketers who had their careers interrupted by the outbreak of the Second World War but he did manage to make some first-class appearances during the conflict. Whilst serving in India, he played for the Services XI against an Indian XI in the Brabourne Stadium, Bombay. The Nottinghamshire batsman showed his pedigree by making a second-innings score of 129. County team-mate Harold Butler was also in the Services side and picked up four wickets in the match.

FRIDAY 14th FEBRUARY 1896

Nottinghamshire's Charles Wright, a right-handed batsman who finished with a modest career average of just 15.88, nevertheless played in three Test matches for England. His debut came as one of nine newcomers in the side, against South Africa at Port Elizabeth. In a game which only lasted for two days, he made scores of 19 and 33, batting at nine in the first innings and opening in the second. Although his achievements were considerable in a low-scoring contest, he was completely outdone by George Lohmann of Surrey who ended the match with a hat-trick and figures of 8-7 – a new best for Test cricket – as the South Africans were bowled out for just 30.

DEREK RANDALL, NOTTINGHAMSHIRE'S 'GREAT ENTERTAINER'

SATURDAY 14th FEBRUARY 2004

During the first of two spells with Nottinghamshire, Bilal Shafayat earned selection for an England A tour of India and Malaysia. He made two appearances, beginning with a four-day contest in Chennai against Tamil Nadu. Playing as a wicketkeeper/batsman, Shafayat scored 41 and 27 and claimed three dismissals. Notts team-mate Kevin Pietersen retired hurt in the first innings, having scored 147.

WEDNESDAY 15th FEBRUARY 1984

Derek Randall scored seven centuries for England in his 47 Tests. The final one came in his 43rd match – against New Zealand at Eden Park, Auckland. Responding to the home team's 496-9 declared, England ensured that the match would be drawn by replying with 439, Randall scoring 104.

WEDNESDAY 16th FEBRUARY 1831

Alfred Clarke, the son of the Trent Bridge founder William Clarke, was born in Nottingham and followed his father's enthusiasm for the sport of cricket. He made 24 appearances for Nottinghamshire and was usually available when called upon to make up the numbers in the All England Eleven. A right-handed batsman, his top career score was only 57.

THURSDAY 16th FEBRUARY 1933

Winning to go 3-1 up in the series, England regained the Ashes after a six-wicket victory over Australia at the Gabba in Brisbane. Nottinghamshire's Harold Larwood, the spearhead behind the controversial Bodyline tactics, took seven wickets in the match.

SATURDAY 17th FEBRUARY 1883

Although it was to be his fourth and final appearance for England, Nottinghamshire's Fred Morley played in a match that remains unique to this day. The last Test at the SCG had an unusual experiment, with a different wicket being used for each of the four innings. Although the respective scores, 263, 262, 197 and 199-6 were relatively similar, the Australians came out on top to level the series at 2-2. Morley, a left-arm fast bowler, took just two wickets in the contest to conclude his international career with 16 scalps to his name.

SATURDAY 17th FEBRUARY 1912

Tom Bokenham Reddick was born in Shanghai and was taught to play cricket with the help of the family's Chinese staff. Brought up in England, his skills were polished under the tutelage of former South African Test all-rounder Aubrey Faulkner. Reddick later played twice for Middlesex before joining the Royal Air Force during the war. Settling in Worksop when peace returned, he made 50 first-class appearances for Notts, scoring 2,225 runs at 31.78. After two seasons on the Trent Bridge staff he emigrated to Cape Town, where he died in 1982, aged 70.

TUESDAY 18th FEBRUARY 1941

George Jasper Groves died in Newmarket, Suffolk, at the age of 72. He made 17 appearances for Nottinghamshire during the 1899 and 1900 seasons but without achieving more than moderate success. A middle-order batsman, he totalled 584 runs with just two half-centuries and a best of 56 not out, scored against Kent at Trent Bridge.

FRIDAY 19th FEBRUARY 2010

Two Nottinghamshire players were at the forefront of an impressive England success in a Twenty20 international against Pakistan in Dubai's Sport City Stadium. Off-spinner Graeme Swann took 2-18 from three overs, with county colleague Stuart Broad collecting 2-23 from four overs, as well as picking up three catches in the outfield. Fittingly, their contributions helped set up a comfortable seven-wicket victory.

SUNDAY 20th FEBRUARY 1949

Born in Leamington Spa, Edward Ernest "Eddie" Hemmings had already played in 177 first-class matches for Warwickshire before joining Notts in 1979. Having begun his career as a right-arm medium-pacer, the decision to switch to bowling off-spin reaped handsome dividends. As well as helping his new side to County Championship success in both 1981 and 1987, Hemmings also became a Test match cricketer at the age of 33 – representing his country in 16 matches at that level, as well as in 33 ODIs. For Nottinghamshire, the spinner became a prolific wicket-taker and consistent match-winner, eventually capturing 850 first-class wickets for the county, at an average of 27.86, with a best of 7-23. He also scored 4,366 runs at 17.74. He took a further 263 List A wickets in 268 matches.

SATURDAY 20th FEBRUARY 1897

Trent Bridge has played host to England on numerous occasions at cricket – and once at football. The full international saw the home nation defeat Ireland by six goals to nil, with an estimated crowd of 14,000 seeing debutant Fred Wheldon of Aston Villa bag a hat-trick. His club team-mate, Charlie Athersmith, also scored, with Derby County's Steve Bloomer getting the other two goals.

WEDNESDAY 21st FEBRUARY 1900

John D'Ewes Evelyn Firth only enjoyed the briefest of first-class careers before becoming a Church of England clergyman. A leg-break and googly bowler, he was born on this day and achieved fleeting fame as a student at Winchester College. After taking all ten wickets in an innings against Eton College (for 41) in 1917 he was listed as one of the Wisden Cricketers of the Year in the 1918 almanack. Nicknamed "Budge", he played twice for Nottinghamshire in 1919 before opting to take an alternative choice of career.

SATURDAY 22nd FEBRUARY 1873

Born in Ruddington, George Lutha Robinson was a right-handed batsman and leg-break bowler who appeared for his county side on five occasions, taking just one wicket and scoring a total of 58 runs. He died at Conisbrough in Yorkshire on 23rd March 1930.

MONDAY 23rd FEBRUARY 1959

Kevin Saxelby was a hard-working fast bowler who appeared in 136 first-class matches for Nottinghamshire between 1978 and 1990. Born in Worksop, he made his debut for the county at home to Leicestershire, picking up Chris Balderstone as the first of exactly 300 wickets that he would eventually take for the county. Those wickets came at 32.56 each with a best return of 6-49. He made just three championship appearances in the 1981 title-winning side but made a far greater impact six years later, taking 47 wickets from 19 matches as the pennant again returned to Trent Bridge. Saxelby played in 162 List A matches, picking up a further 224 dismissals, with six five-wicket hauls, and appeared in the Lord's finals of 1985 and 1987. Younger brother Mark also played for the county, whilst cousin David and nephew Ian both appeared for the second XI.

SATURDAY 24th FEBRUARY 1951

One of Nottinghamshire's greatest-ever entertainers was born in Retford. Derek William Randall played for the county for more than two decades, displaying the same enthusiasm in his 40s as he had as a youngster. The right-handed batsman scored more than 23,000 first-class runs for Notts, averaging 38.32, and notched up almost 11,000 more in one-day matches. Affectionately nicknamed either "Rags" or "Arkle", he was an outstanding fielder and solely responsible for running out countless batsmen with his athleticism and accuracy. One flash of his brilliance would light up an entire day's play. Forty-seven Tests brought seven centuries, his highest the 174 he scored in the Melbourne Centenary Test of 1977. Randall played in four Lord's finals for Notts and the 1979 ICC World Cup Final with England.

SATURDAY 25th FEBRUARY 1933

When you've spent an entire series giving opposition batsmen a diet of fast, short-pitched, rib-tickling deliveries you would have thought that Harold Larwood wouldn't have wanted to put himself back in the firing line to perhaps face some of his own medicine. None of it though – with the Notts man happily going in as night-watchman, on the second evening of the fifth Test between Australia and England, at Sydney. Five not out overnight, Larwood went on to reach 98 before being cruelly dismissed by Philip Lee when two short of a maiden Test century. This turned out to be the final innings that he would play in Test cricket.

THURSDAY 25th FEBRUARY 1965

Although born in Lancashire, Michael Newell became part of the scenery at Trent Bridge after making his debut for the Nottinghamshire second team whilst only 16. The right-handed batsman graduated to the first XI in 1984 and went on to make 102 first-class appearances and another 40 outings in List A cricket. His highest career score was an unbeaten 203, made against Derbyshire at the County Ground in 1987. Newell scored 1,054 runs that season, as Nottinghamshire won the County Championship. By the time of their next two triumphs, in 2005 and 2010, Newell had graduated from being a member of the coaching staff to become their director of cricket.

THURSDAY 25th FEBRUARY 1971

Australian leg-spinner Stuart Charles Glyndwr MacGill took 122 wickets in just 32 first-class appearances for Nottinghamshire, between 2002 and 2004. Born in Western Australia, his Test outings suffered due to playing in the same era as Shane Warne but he was a proven match-winner, particularly in county cricket, where he bagged eight five-wicket hauls.

WEDNESDAY 26th FEBRUARY 1851

Mordecai Sherwin was born at Greasley, north-west of Nottingham. A wicketkeeper, he played 328 first-class matches, 206 of them for Nottinghamshire. With 500 dismissals (387 catches and 113 stumpings) he ranks sixth on the county's list of keepers and he played three Tests for England. Sherwin also kept goal for Notts County and later became a publican, dying at his residence, The Craven Arms on Woodborough Road, in 1910.

FRIDAY 27th FEBRUARY 1920

An elegant and stylish opening batsman, Reginald Thomas Simpson was born in Sherwood and went on to score 23,088 runs for Nottinghamshire, with 48 centuries and a top score of 243 not out. He played for England on 27 occasions, captained Notts between 1951 and 1960 and carried on playing for another three years before retiring to become a member of the county committee.

SATURDAY 27th FEBRUARY 1965

David James Millns had two spells on the staff at Trent Bridge, playing a total of 24 first-class and 12 one-day matches. A right-arm quick bowler and left-handed lower-order batsman, he was born in Clipstone and played the bulk of his career at Leicestershire, before returning to Nottinghamshire in 2000 for his final season at county level.

FRIDAY 28th FEBRUARY 1941

Right-handed batsman Harry "Ian" Moore scored seven centuries for Nottinghamshire, with a personal best of 203 not out, scored against the touring Indians in 1967. Born in Sleaford, he appeared in 176 first-class matches for Notts, amassing 6,735 runs. He also appeared in 15 List A matches before leaving to play Minor Counties cricket with Lincolnshire. Moore was 69 when he died in 2010.

REG SIMPSON, NOTTS CAPTAIN FROM 1951 TO 1960

TUESDAY 28th FEBRUARY 1978

Dismissed in the first innings for a duck by soon-to-be Notts team-mate Richard Hadlee, Derek Randall made his unwanted way on to a short list of unusual Test dismissals in the second innings against New Zealand at Lancaster Park in Christchurch. Having reached 13, he was adjudged to have been run out by the bowler, Ewen Chatfield, who suddenly, without warning or reaching his delivery stride, stopped and whipped off the bails underarm. This mode of dismissal (Mankading) had only occurred twice before – and once since – in Tests. The incident was greatly deplored and caused a temporary strain on relations between the two sides.

FRIDAY 29th FEBRUARY 1856

Walter Wright was born in Hucknall Torkard, Nottinghamshire, and was originally registered at birth as Walter Shooter. As a left-arm fast-medium bowler, Wright's first opportunity with the county came in 1879 when he appeared against Lancashire at Trent Bridge. That was the first of 72 appearances for Notts, which brought 193 wickets. His best performance with the ball was 8-53 against Sussex at Hove. A lower-order, right-handed batsman, he only passed 50 twice, although the best knock of his career extended as far as an unbeaten 127 against Gloucestershire in 1883. Aside from his cricket, Wright was an outstanding sprinter, ranked as the second fastest in the world at one stage. He turned to football in later life, coaching both Reading and Swindon Town. Moving to Lancashire, he became coach and groundsman at Leigh Cricket Club and he made his home in that town and died there in March 1940, at the age of 84.

SUNDAY 29th FEBRUARY 1976

Garnet Morley Lee died in Newark on this day, aged 89. Between 1910 and 1922 he played in 140 first-class matches for Nottinghamshire, scoring 4,988 runs with six centuries. The highest score of his career came when batting against Leicestershire at Trent Bridge in 1913 when he reached 200 not out. A right-handed batsman, he was also a respected leg-break and googly bowler who took 73 wickets for the county. Garnet went on to make 229 first-class appearances for Derbyshire and later served as a first-class umpire.

NOTTINGHAMSHIRE CCC
On This Day

MARCH

SATURDAY 1st MARCH 1958

Beginning the morning on 228 not out, Garfield Sobers made this a record-breaking day to remember. Playing against Pakistan at Sabina Park, Kingston, Jamaica, the left-hander took his score to an undefeated 365, surpassing Len Hutton's 364 as the highest Test match score of all time. Sobers would not only still hold the record when he joined Nottinghamshire a decade later, he would keep it until 1994 when another West Indian, Brian Lara, would set a new individual milestone.

FRIDAY 2nd MARCH 1877

Thomas Barker first played for Nottingham in 1821 and was a member of the side that played Sussex in the first county match 14 years later. Born in Calverton, he was regarded as one of the quickest bowlers of his time and was the first Nottingham professional to appear in the Gentlemen v Players series of matches. In 14 games for Nottinghamshire, Barker took 51 wickets but the latter stages of his career were hampered by a serious leg injury, sustained after he fell out of a horse-drawn carriage whilst crossing London. He lived there later, after being engaged by Lord's as an umpire, but would return to his home city each winter to work as a stockiner.

MONDAY 2nd MARCH 2009

Samit Patel's maiden first-class century, outside the UK, came whilst playing for the England Lions against New Zealand A at the Queenstown Events Centre, Otago. The Nottinghamshire batsman scored 101, from 139 balls, with 16 fours in the drawn four-day match.

WEDNESDAY 2nd MARCH 2011

Kevin O'Brien didn't have too many opportunities to impress during his brief stint as a Nottinghamshire player in 2009. He played in just one first-class game, five Twenty20 matches and eight List A games, where his top score was only 42. Should anyone be in doubt of his abilities though, they would have been suitably impressed by the performance of the Irishman at the ICC World Cup. Playing against England on this day in Bangalore, O'Brien scored a match-winning 113, with his century coming from just 50 deliveries, and containing 13 boundaries and six huge maximums.

SATURDAY 3rd MARCH 1990

Nottinghamshire's Andy Afford made the first of his two appearances for England A. Playing against Zimbabwe at the Harare Sports Club, the left-arm spinner took four wickets in the five-day match (2-58 and 2-18) as England completed a ten-wicket victory.

TUESDAY 3rd MARCH 2009

Former Nottinghamshire and England opening batsman Chris Broad was caught up in a terrorist attack in Lahore which left eight people dead. Travelling behind the Sri Lankan team coach, which was en route to the Gaddafi Stadium to face Pakistan in a Test, referee Broad, plus the other officials, came under fire from a dozen masked gunmen.

SATURDAY 4th MARCH 1950

Born in Derby, Howard "Trevor" Tunnicliffe made 65 first-class appearances for Nottinghamshire between 1973 and 1980. A right-handed batsman, he scored 2,116 runs at 25.49 with his only century coming against Middlesex at Trent Bridge. A right-arm medium-paced bowler, he captured 42 wickets, with a best of 4-30. In one-day competition Tunnicliffe made 104 appearances, scored 1,068 runs and took 45 wickets.

WEDNESDAY 4th MARCH 1992

Paul Johnson celebrated his first overseas one-day appearance for England A by collecting the man of the match award after a six-wicket victory over Barbados at the Kensington Oval, Bridgetown. Johnson took three catches in the outfield as the home side reached 171-9 and then guided his side to victory with a score of 56 before being dismissed by Vasbert Drakes, who would become a Trent Bridge team-mate in 1999.

SUNDAY 5th MARCH 1876

James "Jimmy" Iremonger was born in Norton, Yorkshire, and went on to become an outstanding servant to Notts, playing 344 matches between 1899 and 1914. The right-handed batsman scored 16,622 runs, with 31 centuries and a highest score of 272. He also took 596 wickets with his medium-paced bowling, with a best of 8-21. Iremonger played football for Nottingham Forest and won three England caps. He was 80 when he died in West Bridgford.

FRIDAY 5th MARCH 1999

In a bid to try and make one-day cricket more 'trendy' and marketable, the ECB asked the counties to come up with a suitable nickname for their sides. The release of those names introduced us to the likes of the Essex Eagles, Sussex Sharks and Notts Outlaws. Revealing how the Trent Bridge side had come up with their new name, Paul Johnson, a mainstay of the Notts batting at the time, said: "I was asked for my opinion on us becoming the 'Hoods'. I pointed out that the American Football League team in the city had the same name and suggested 'Outlaws' instead. After a brief discussion it was unanimously decided that we'd become the 'Outlaws'."

THURSDAY 6th MARCH 1884

Famed for just one outstanding innings, Edwin Boaler "Ted" Alletson was born in Welbeck. His scintillating 189 against Sussex in May 1911 was the exception, rather than the rule, as it was his only first-class century in 119 matches. Alletson played for Nottinghamshire between 1906 and 1914, scoring 3,217 runs. Capable of bowling either medium-pace or leg-break deliveries, he picked up 33 wickets, with a best of 6-74. He died in 1963, aged 79.

TUESDAY 7th MARCH 1876

Born in Hyson Green in 1940, Samuel Biddulph had few equals as a wicketkeeper after graduating into the county side. He played in 76 first-class matches, scoring 983 runs and completing 116 dismissals but was only 35 when he took ill and died of kidney disease, being buried in the General Cemetery in Nottingham.

WEDNESDAY 7th MARCH 1888

A "round-arm, left-arm fast bowler", James Coupe "Jemmy" Shaw provided a formidable opponent for batsmen up and down the country during the 11 years he played for Nottinghamshire. In 115 matches, from his debut in 1865 to his final match in 1875, he took 642 wickets at an average of just 14.41. His most prolific season with the ball came in 1870 when he took 97 wickets. The following year produced a further 90, including a career-best 9-86. Aged just 51, Shaw died on this day of pneumonia at his home at Sutton-in-Ashfield.

FRIDAY 7th MARCH 1975

Northampton-born Andy Oram made 19 first-class appearances for Notts in 1997 and 1998. As a right-arm medium-pace bowler he took 57 wickets at 29 runs each, with a best of 4-37. He also took 23 wickets in 20 limited-overs matches.

SATURDAY 8th MARCH 2008

Against New Zealand, at Hamilton, Ryan Sidebottom became the 11th Englishman to take a Test hat-trick. Stephen Fleming, a former Nottinghamshire county team-mate, was the left-arm pace bowler's first victim, splendidly caught by Alastair Cook. Matthew Sinclair followed in exactly the same fashion before Jacob Oram was given out lbw. Despite Sidebottom's ten wickets in the match, the home side still triumphed by 189 runs.

SUNDAY 9th MARCH 1947

Born in Windsor, Richard Bielby was a right-handed batsman who was given a first-team debut by Notts in 1967 but he struggled to establish himself, making only 43 first-class appearances in five years – one of them the 'Sobers' match at Swansea in 1968. Bielby only made two 50s for the county before being released at the end of the 1971 campaign.

TUESDAY 10th MARCH 1992

Considered a little unfortunate not to receive full international recognition, Nottinghamshire's Paul Johnson did make five first-class and three one-day appearances for the England A side during his career. His highest score of 71 came against Trinidad and Tobago at Guaracara Park, Pointe-a-Pierre.

SUNDAY 11th MARCH 1894

Former Test batsman John Selby died in Nottingham after suffering a paralytic stroke. Registered as John Burrows at birth, he was given his county debut by Notts in 1870, when he was just a month short of his 21st birthday. Selby went on two tours of Australia with MCC, playing in six Test matches and also went on a tour of Canada and North America in 1879. He scored a total of 6,215 first-class runs from a total of 222 appearances, playing his final game in 1887.

WEDNESDAY 12th MARCH 1913

Either side of the Second World War, the Nottinghamshire attack relied heavily upon the accuracy and seam movement of Harold James Butler. Born in Clifton, he made his debut for the county in 1933 and took career-best figures of 8-15 against Surrey four years later. Butler served in India during the conflict but returned to make two Test appearances, one against South Africa at The Oval and one in the Caribbean against the West Indies. In 319 first-class matches he claimed a total of 952 wickets, 919 of them for Notts. He died in July 1991 in Lenton, aged 78.

THURSDAY 12th MARCH 1953

Hard-hitting opening batsman Paul Todd was born at Morton, near Southwell. His Nottinghamshire debut came towards the end of the 1972 season when he appeared against Warwickshire at Trent Bridge, making 66 before being forced to retire hurt with a broken jaw after being hit by a delivery from AC Smith. Over the course of the next decade he played in a total of 156 first-class matches for Notts, scoring 7,168 runs at an average of 27.56. His highest score came against Gloucestershire in 1975 at Trent Bridge, when he made 178. Todd also played in 129 List A matches, compiling a career tally of 2,452 runs. After five years away from the county scene, the right-hander returned to play one season for Glamorgan in 1987.

SUNDAY 13th MARCH 1921

Cyril John Poole was born in Forest Town and wrote his name into the sporting record books at an early age by turning out for Mansfield Town against New Brighton on 27 February 1937 becoming, at 15 years 351 days, the youngest to ever appear for the Stags. The left-sided player – either in defence or midfield – was also a very accomplished left-handed batsman and he went on to make 366 first-class appearances for Nottinghamshire, which produced 18,685 runs at 32.49, with 24 centuries and a best of 222 not out. During the winter of 1951-52 Poole was selected for England's tour of India, where he picked up his three Test match caps. In 1996, he passed away at his home in Balderton, aged 74.

THURSDAY 14th MARCH 1991

Born in Mansfield, Jacob Timothy "Jake" Ball played Test, one-day international and Twenty20 cricket for England's Under-19 side before making his first appearance in the Nottinghamshire team with a NatWest Pro40 league outing against Sussex, at Hove in 2009. The right-arm medium-pacer delivered six overs which brought him the wicket of Rory Hamilton-Brown but he made a first-ball duck with the bat. His first-class debut came in the champion county versus MCC match in Abu Dhabi in March 2011. Ball is the nephew of former Nottinghamshire and England wicketkeeper Bruce French.

THURSDAY 15th MARCH 1877

Playing in the first 'recognised' Test, against Australia at the Melbourne Cricket Ground, England included two Nottinghamshire players in their side. One of them, Alfred Shaw, bowled the first delivery in Test cricket – and claimed figures of 5-38 in the home side's second innings. John Selby, also of Notts, was forced into action as an emergency wicketkeeper after the tourists' first choice, Ted Pooley, had been detained by the authorities for assaulting someone who refused to pay a gambling debt, when the side stopped off en route in New Zealand.

WEDNESDAY 16th MARCH 1977

The Centenary Test in Melbourne produced an Australian win by 45 runs, exactly the same victory margin as the original match 100 years earlier. Despite his side's loss, the match was an individual triumph for Nottinghamshire's Derek Randall who scored 174 in the second innings, his highest score on England duty.

SATURDAY 17th MARCH 1849

The lesser-known of the three William Clarkes who played for Nottinghamshire was born in Kirkby-in-Ashfield, where he was always known as "Cricketer Clarke". No relation to the man who turned his meadow into Trent Bridge, the youngest of the three only played half a dozen times, as a left-handed bat and right-arm fast bowler, taking a meagre four wickets with the ball and failing to improve on a best score of 17 with the bat. After his six appearances for the county he went on to become the cricket professional at the Royal Artillery in Woolwich. Clarke died in Mapperley in 1935, aged 86.

FRIDAY 18th MARCH 2011

Having played only five first-class matches, including three whilst on loan at Essex, Nottinghamshire's Andrew Carter received a surprise call to bolster the England Lions squad, on tour in the Caribbean. With Surrey's Jade Dernbach then summoned to join the full England World Cup party in the sub-continent, Carter was allowed to take his place on the second day of a four-day match against the Windward Islands in Roseau, Dominica. Carter took 2-33 from the 16 overs he bowled in the match and scored five not out in his only innings.

SATURDAY 19th MARCH 1994

The man who captained Nottinghamshire to their 2005 County Championship success won 111 Test caps for New Zealand. Stephen Fleming's first appearance at the highest level came in Hamilton, against India. The left-hander kicked off his long period of international success with scores of 16 and 92 in a drawn contest.

WEDNESDAY 20th MARCH 1940

Henry Richardson was a right-arm medium-pace bowler who appeared 53 times for Nottinghamshire between 1887 and 1890. He claimed seven five-wicket hauls for the county, with a best of 7-24, which came against Middlesex at Lord's. Richardson had been born at Bulwell in 1857 and died there, aged 82.

TUESDAY 20th MARCH 1973

South African Test match spinner Nicky Boje played 20 times for Nottinghamshire in 2002. Born in Bloemfontein, the slow left-armer took 27 wickets in nine first-class games and a further 13 in his 11 List A appearances. In championship cricket he top-scored with 84 and went a little better in the one-day game, scoring 86 against Leicestershire at Trent Bridge.

MONDAY 20th MARCH 1989

Born in Chittagong, Tamim Iqbal became the first international cricketer from Bangladesh to play for Nottinghamshire when he made five appearances for the Outlaws in the Twenty20 competition in 2011. The aggressive, left-handed opening batsman scored 104 runs with a top score of 47, which came against Yorkshire Carnegie at Headingley.

FRIDAY 21st MARCH 1890

Born in Underwood, Nottinghamshire, William Arthur "Bill" Flint was a good enough all-rounder to score three first-class centuries and take 236 wickets. He played for Nottinghamshire for a decade from 1919, ending his stint with the county after playing in five championship matches during their 1929 title-winning campaign. His tally of 3,345 runs came at an average of 19.33, with his wickets being taken at 29.51 and a best of 6-23.

SATURDAY 22nd MARCH 2008

Fittingly, for a man who had just taken his best figures in Test match cricket, Ryan Sidebottom won the man of the match award after England's 121-run success over New Zealand in Napier. The Nottinghamshire quick bowler claimed 7-47 in the Kiwis' first innings, including the wicket of former county colleague Stephen Fleming.

MONDAY 23rd MARCH 1885

Nottinghamshire's Arthur Shrewsbury had a double cause for celebration after scoring 105 not out for England against Australia in the fifth and final Test of the rubber at the Melbourne Cricket Ground. Skippering his country, he not only became the first England captain to score a Test match hundred but his performance helped set up a win by an innings and 98 runs – thereby sealing the series 3-2 after the opening four matches had been shared.

FRIDAY 24th MARCH 1899

William "Billy" Barnes was considered to be one of the finest all-rounders of his generation. From his Nottinghamshire debut in 1875 he was a virtual ever-present for the next 18 years, scoring 8,328 runs and taking 435 wickets. The highest of his 13 centuries was 160 and his best analysis with the ball was 8-64. Eleven of his 21 Test appearances were on home soil, with the other ten all in Australia, spread over three different tours. His only international hundred came at Adelaide in 1885, with a score of 134. From 1895 to 1898 he was employed on the MCC groundstaff and appeared as a first-class umpire. Having worked as a cotton weaver earlier in life, Barnes then took over as landlord of the Angel Inn, Mansfield Woodhouse, where he passed away, aged 47.

FRIDAY 24th MARCH 1944

A real "Basher" was born in Nairobi, Kenya. Sheikh Basharat Hassan joined Nottinghamshire in 1966, making his debut as wicketkeeper in a fixture at The Parks against Oxford University. Over the next couple of years his appearances were limited due to him having to meet the various residency qualifications but he then established himself as a top-order batsman of some prowess. In 329 matches between 1966 and 1985, he scored over 14,000 runs, with a best score of 182 not out. He scored an additional 6,842 runs from 285 List A matches. After retiring from the game, "Basher" served as a first-class umpire before returning to Trent Bridge to work in a variety of administrative roles within the club.

SATURDAY 24th MARCH 1979

Graeme Peter Swann established himself as the number one spin bowler in world cricket's one-day rankings during 2011. Born in Northampton, he made one solitary England ODI appearance when with his home county but after switching to Trent Bridge in 2005 further success came along more rapidly. He was a member of the Nottinghamshire side that won the County Championship in 2005 and returned to the international fold in 2007. His first Test appearance was in India in 2008 and two years later Swann was a member of his country's successful ICC Twenty20-winning team.

THURSDAY 25th MARCH 1909

Right-handed batsman Ron Taylor made 23 first-class appearances for Notts in the 1930s. Born in The Meadows, he scored 11 on debut, against Northamptonshire at Worksop. He scored a total of 599 runs for the county, at an average of just over 18, figures boosted by his one career century, an innings of 107 versus Sussex at Trent Bridge in 1934. Taylor, a cousin of Lancashire and England player George Duckworth, was 77 when he died in Nottingham in 1986.

TUESDAY 25th MARCH 1930

Nottinghamshire's George Gunn only managed one century on the 1929-30 MCC tour of the West Indies. Batting in the second innings of a drawn match against Jamaica in Kingston, he scored 178, sharing in an opening stand of 322 with Surrey's Andy Sandham, who scored 155.

MONDAY 26th MARCH 1860

They always say it's better to have played once than never at all but it will remain a mystery as to why Joseph Pearson only made one first-class appearance for Nottinghamshire. A member of the Worksop club, the town of his birth, he twice played in the Colts v the County matches that were often used to identify promising young talent. His opportunity came with a trip to The Oval in 1883 to face Surrey. The home side were already seven wickets down when Alf Shaw tossed the ball to the debutant – who quickly proceeded to wrap up the innings with figures of 3.1-2-1-3. Pearson's only other contribution in the drawn match was in making a single run. He didn't appear again, returning to club cricket – and he died in Boughton, Notts in 1892, aged just 31.

SATURDAY 27th MARCH 1880

George Jarvis was regarded as one of the leading Nottingham batsmen of his day and gained recognition by playing in the inaugural North v South fixture and also in a number of Gentlemen v Players fixtures. His total number of first-class outings can be assessed as 37, during which he amassed 814 runs and took nine wickets. Charles Jarvis, his brother, played four times for the Nottingham club but died well before George, who passed away on this day, just short of his 80th birthday.

FRIDAY 27th MARCH 2009

David Hussey took the man of the match honours and played a starring role for Australia against South Africa in a Twenty20 international at Johannesburg. The Nottinghamshire batsman plundered a rapid 88 not out from just 44 deliveries, with five fours and six maximums. For good measure, he then took 2-21 with the ball, although the home nation managed to scrape to victory in the final over.

SATURDAY 28th MARCH 1992

At Kensington Oval in Bridgetown, Barbados, Nottinghamshire were represented by both Paul Johnson and Andy Pick in the England A side that played against their West Indies counterparts. Johnson made scores of 43 and 9, with Pick taking 2-46 and 0-14 in the drawn contest.

SATURDAY 29th MARCH 1947

Born in Kirkby-in-Ashfield in 1867, Sam Lowe played once for Nottinghamshire, before going on to create a little piece of Glamorgan history. Brother of Richard, who played for Sussex, and Tom, who also made just one Notts appearance, Sam played against Lancashire at Old Trafford in 1894. He scored 8 and 0, and failed to take a wicket in a convincing defeat. Looking for opportunities elsewhere, Sam joined Cardiff as their professional and found his way into the Glamorgan side that played in the Minor Counties championship. Their first ever victory was against Cornwall at Swansea in 1897 and during it, Lowe recorded a hat-trick, the first by a Glamorgan player. He passed away, aged 79, back in Kirkby-in-Ashfield.

TUESDAY 30th MARCH 1954

Garfield Sobers was only 17 when he made his Test debut, against England in Jamaica. Batting at number nine in the order, he made 14 not out and 26 and recorded figures of 4-75 and 0-6 (bowling just one over) with the ball. His side were easily defeated but – fully 14 years before he would join Nottinghamshire – the West Indies had found a new talent who would soon become a global superstar.

THURSDAY 31st MARCH 1983

Hashim Amla was born in Durban, South Africa, and he had risen to number two in the ICC Test rankings when he was offered the chance to join Nottinghamshire for a brief spell at the start of the 2010 season. He scored 86 against Durham MCCU on his debut and 127 on his first championship appearance, against Kent at Trent Bridge and in just seven first-class innings he averaged over 77.

NOTTINGHAMSHIRE CCC
On This Day

APRIL

WEDNESDAY 1st APRIL 1964

Born in Crewe, John Edward Morris was 36 by the time of his Nottinghamshire debut in 2000. The former Derbyshire, Durham and England batsman scored 1,241 runs in 21 championship appearances for Notts before announcing his retirement after a win over his first county, Derbyshire, in August 2001.

FRIDAY 1st APRIL 2011

Nottinghamshire collected some silverware when they won the Emirates Airlines T20 competition, played at 7he Sevens Ground in Dubai. In the semi-final they defeated an MCC side, led by former Indian Test captain Saurav Ganguly, before taking on Sussex in the final. Chasing a victory target of 142, Notts were guided to an eight-wicket victory thanks to an unbeaten 76 from Samit Patel.

WEDNESDAY 2nd APRIL 1947

Joseph Hardstaff senior died at Nuncargate, Notts, at the age of 64. He made his county debut in 1902 and remained a central figure in the side until he retired at the end of the 1924 season. Hardstaff played in 340 first-class games for Notts, scoring more than 15,000 runs, with a best of 213 not out. Considered unlucky not to have made more than the five Test appearances he was given, he also missed out a little after becoming a well-respected umpire. Having stood in 21 Tests his duties were restricted when his son, Joseph Hardstaff junior, established himself in the England set-up.

FRIDAY 3rd APRIL 1931

Born at Winchmore Hill in Middlesex, David John Halfyard became a Nottinghamshire player thanks to a stroke of good fortune. Ironically, bad luck had prematurely halted his first-class career with Kent after he had been badly hurt in a motoring accident. Having qualified as a first-class umpire, he was observed bowling a few deliveries in the nets at a Notts match and was offered a trial by the county. He went on to make 77 first-class and 38 List A appearances for the county, taking 194 wickets in the longer format and 50 in the shorter, all between the ages of 37 and 39. After retiring to North Devon, he passed away at his home in Northam in 1996.

CHRIS READ HOLDS THE EMIRATES AIRLINES TWENTY20 TROPHY IN DUBAI, 2011

FRIDAY 3rd APRIL 2009

Three legendary cricketers with Nottinghamshire connections were among the 55 inaugural inductees into the ICC Cricket Hall of Fame. Sir Richard Hadlee was the only New Zealander on the list and joined fellow knight Sir Garfield Sobers and ex-Notts and England pace bowler Harold Larwood amongst those elected.

SATURDAY 4th APRIL 1964

Four years before he joined Nottinghamshire, as their first major overseas import and captain, Garfield Sobers was able to show his worth as an all-rounder under the less demanding gaze of the Hong Kong Cricket Club. Touring with the EW Swanton XI, the West Indian produced a stunning display with both bat and ball to defeat a local Hong Kong Select XI almost single-handedly. He scored 106 and followed it up with a devastating spell of 5-19.

FRIDAY 5th APRIL 1974

Shortly before he was due to embark upon his final season of county cricket with Nottinghamshire, Garfield Sobers wound down his Test career. His 93rd and final match at that level came against England in Port-of-Spain, Trinidad. Sadly for the great all-rounder, his last international appearance ended in defeat as England managed to square the series. Sobers bowed out with scores of 0 and 20 but his three wickets in the match meant that he had become the first West Indian to take 100 wickets against England. His entire haul of Test wickets was 235 and he scored 8,032 runs at 57.78 each.

FRIDAY 6th APRIL 1956

Born in Colombo, Gamini Goonesena was one of the first cricketers from Ceylon (now Sri Lanka) to make their mark overseas. The Nottinghamshire all-rounder was often called upon to appear for assorted international and touring sides and he impressed in the Caribbean whilst touring with the EW Swanton XI, which was being captained by England's Colin Cowdrey. At Port-of-Spain, Trinidad, in a five-day first-class match against a strong West Indies XI, Goonesena scored 24 and 45 and took 4-129 (which included the wickets of Clyde Walcott and Rohan Kanhai) and 0-26, although the home side won on the last day by eight wickets.

WEDNESDAY 7th APRIL 1993

Nottinghamshire and Glamorgan have faced each other at several different venues over the years, including this fixture in South Africa. With both counties getting some warm-weather cricket ahead of the English campaign, they played a 35-overs-per-side contest at the Northerns-Goodwood Cricket Club Oval, outside Cape Town. One must assume that Notts weren't properly acclimatised as they lost by 50 runs in a very low-scoring contest. Glamorgan made 121-9 with Notts only mustering 71-6 in reply.

WEDNESDAY 8th APRIL 1959

Franklyn Dacosta Stephenson is widely regarded as the best West Indian never to play a Test. Born in Saint James, Barbados, he joined Notts in 1988 and enjoyed the most sensational of debut seasons. Since the reduction of first-class games in 1969, only one player, New Zealander Richard Hadlee, had achieved the legendary double of 1,000 runs and 100 wickets in first-class cricket. Stephenson's heroics saw him become the second to reach the feat. Renowned for becoming one of the first fast bowlers to develop a truly devilish slower delivery, he played in 82 first-class games for Nottinghamshire over a four-year period which produced 2,845 runs and 349 wickets at an average of 23. He also appeared in 93 List A matches, with a further 1,191 runs and 142 wickets.

SATURDAY 9th APRIL 2011

It's always nice to re-acclimatise whenever you begin playing again on foreign soil. Adam Voges' return to the UK, after a winter in his homeland with Western Australia, couldn't have gone much better. Playing against Oxford University at The Parks, he scored his third – and largest – century for Nottinghamshire, 165 on the opening day of a pre-season friendly. Team-mate Alistair Brown weighed in with an undefeated 128, the 44th and final hundred of his own first-class career.

SATURDAY 10th APRIL 2010

Hashim Amla's first innings in Nottinghamshire colours ended 14 runs short of a century. The South African Test batsman, signed on a short-term deal, made 86 from 128 balls against Durham MCCU at The Racecourse in Durham.

FRIDAY 11th APRIL 1856

Arthur Shrewsbury was born at New Lenton in Nottinghamshire and went on to become one of the best players of his generation. In 358 appearances for Nottinghamshire he scored 19,409 runs at 37.68. The right-hander's top score was 267 – a total he hit twice, against Middlesex in 1887 and v Sussex in 1890. He played for England on 23 occasions in Test matches, captaining the side in seven of them. In tragic circumstances, Shrewsbury took his own life in 1903, at the age of 47. He'd complained of kidney pains the previous September and had visited various specialists who couldn't find anything seriously wrong with him. After visiting a gunsmith to buy a revolver – and then returning to get the correct bullets – he shot himself twice, once in the chest and then, fatally, in the head.

MONDAY 12th APRIL 1999

Left-arm medium-fast bowler David Lucas made his debut for Nottinghamshire against Cambridge University at Trent Bridge. He marked the occasion by taking 3-62 from 22 overs, with all three of them courtesy of successful lbw appeals.

SUNDAY 13th APRIL 1851

Born in Arnold in 1810, Samuel Redgate was a right-arm fast bowler, whose action was described as "graceful". For a period he was rated as the most destructive bowler of his type in the land and his meeting with the premier batsman around, Fuller Pilch, was eagerly anticipated. The pair came face-to-face in a Gentlemen v Players match at Lord's in 1835 and the outcome was decisively won by Redgate who twice clean bowled his rival for a pair. His record of 426 wickets came from just 79 matches but ill health, caused by drink, cut short his career and he was only 41 when he died in Old Radford.

WEDNESDAY 13th APRIL 1955

Roy Evatt Dexter was born in Nottingham and made 22 first-class appearances for Nottinghamshire between 1975 and 1981. A consistently high scorer in second-team cricket, the right-hander was unable to convert that form at the higher level and only scored a total of 464 runs at an average of 15.46.

SUNDAY 13th APRIL 2003

In one of the more unusual dismissals in first-class cricket, Nottinghamshire's Andrew James "AJ" Harris became only the fourth player in history to be timed out. Playing against Durham UCCE at Trent Bridge, the injured Harris wasn't expected to be required to bat. A collapse of late-order wickets left Chris Read unbeaten on 94. Instructed to get ready and get out there to help Read get to his century, Harris eventually made his way out of the pavilion to find the other players returning, the umpires having decided they would wait no longer!

TUESDAY 14th APRIL 1896

John Chapman was the step-son of the Trent Bridge founder William Clarke. Born in Nottingham in 1814, he moved to the Trent Bridge Inn with his mother, Mary Chapman, in 1821. He played 13 times for Notts, top-scoring with 41 in 1843. Chapman took over the running of the ground once Clarke had moved to London but lost £40 on staging a match in 1848 and decided to move to Gainsborough, where he set up a vet's practice and remained there until his death in 1896, aged 81.

TUESDAY 15th APRIL 1873

Joseph Guy was 59 when he died at his home, the Carpenter's Arms on Mansfield Road, Nottingham. He had purchased the public house with proceeds from his benefit match in 1856. A defensively-minded right-handed batsman, he made his Nottinghamshire debut against Sussex at Brighton in 1837. Over the next couple of decades Guy only made 28 first-class appearances for the county but was a regular for MCC, England and William Clarke's All England Eleven.

FRIDAY 15th APRIL 2011

Nottinghamshire made the most sporting of gestures in their home championship fixture against Hampshire. Visiting wicketkeeper Nic Pothas had injured himself and was unfit for the second day of the match. Notts offered and allowed their academy keeper Adeel Shafique to keep for the opposition. With approval by both umpires and the ECB, the 17-year-old kept impeccably for Hampshire for the entire morning session until replacement Michael Bates arrived.

TUESDAY 15th APRIL 1980

Aged just 40, Barry Stead died on this day at Drighlington, Yorkshire, the county where he played his early cricket. He moved to Trent Bridge in 1962 and in 215 matches for Nottinghamshire took 604 wickets at an average of just 28. The left-arm quick bowler was considered unlucky to be overlooked for international recognition, particularly during the 1972 season when he took 98 first-class wickets. Two years later Stead's wholehearted approach to the game was acknowledged when he won the Professional Cricketers' Association Player of the Year Award. In 1976 he was given a benefit season and, fittingly, bowed out after a match against his first county at Bradford.

SUNDAY 16th APRIL 2006

An explosive innings by Mark Ealham earned him the Walter Lawrence Trophy for scoring the fastest century of the season. The former Test all-rounder scored 112 not out for county champions Nottinghamshire in the traditional curtain-raising match at the start of the new season, against MCC at Lord's. Ealham's explosive knock came from just 53 balls in 56 minutes, with 11 fours and eight sixes. His hundred had come from just 45 balls in 50 minutes.

SATURDAY 17th APRIL 1976

Born in York, wicketkeeper/batsman David Alleyne began his career with Middlesex before moving to Notts in 2005. In his two-year stay at Trent Bridge he played 17 first-class matches, claimed 50 dismissals and scored 701 runs, at an average of 30.47 and with a top score of 109, made against Warwickshire. Alleyne also appeared in eight List A and six Twenty20 matches for the county.

TUESDAY 17th APRIL 2001

Even before he had made his first-class debut for Nottinghamshire, Kevin Pietersen gave a glimpse of his abilities by hitting 115 not out in a pre-season friendly at home to Northamptonshire. The new addition to the Trent Bridge staff shared in a swashbuckling unbroken stand of 294 for the fifth wicket with the vastly more experienced Paul Johnson, who powered his way to a typically brutal 168.

MARK EALHAM, WALTER LAWRENCE TROPHY WINNER IN 2006

MONDAY 18th APRIL 1932

Richard Green Hardstaff took exactly 100 wickets for Nottinghamshire in 30 matches between 1893 and 1899. Having been born in Selston, he played in the Lancashire League for Rawtenstall, before returning to feature for his home county. His best performances with bat and ball came in the same fixture, against Derbyshire at Derby in 1896. As the last man he scored 60 in a stand of 109 with William Gunn (209) and then took 8-53 with his left-arm medium-pace. He retired back to Selston, where he died aged 69.

SATURDAY 18th APRIL 1987

Slow left-arm spinner Graeme Geoffrey White was born in Milton Keynes and began his career with Northants before moving to Trent Bridge ahead of the 2010 season. Establishing himself in List A and Twenty20 cricket with the Outlaws, he only made one championship appearance in his first season but featured in a run of games towards the end of the 2011 campaign, taking his first four-wicket haul for the county and scoring an impressive half-century in a win over Lancashire at Southport.

MONDAY 18th APRIL 1994

The world Test record was broken on this day at the St John's Recreation Ground in Antigua. Former Nottinghamshire star Sir Garfield Sobers had held the record since 1958, when he scored 365 not out for the West Indies against Pakistan. Brian Charles Lara, who hailed from Trinidad and Tobago, went past Sobers' score when he pulled a ball from Nottinghamshire's Chris Lewis, playing for England, away for four. Lara was dismissed shortly afterwards for 375.

TUESDAY 19th APRIL 1966

Paul John Reiffel was born in Box Hill, Victoria, Australia. The right-arm quick bowler played in 35 Tests for his country between 1992 and 1998 and made 92 ODI appearances. In 2000 Reiffel played in seven first-class matches for Nottinghamshire, scoring 275 runs with a best of 74. He also took 21 wickets at an average of 27.9. Known as "Pistol", he also played in nine List A matches for the county, claiming eight wickets.

SATURDAY 20th APRIL 2002

On the opening day of the first-class season Nottinghamshire's Kevin Pietersen and Guy Welton shared in a fourth-wicket stand of 205 against Durham UCCE. Pietersen scored 133 from 148 balls, with his partner making 97. Both were dismissed by the left-arm spin of Rob Ferley, who later spent two seasons on the Notts staff.

TUESDAY 21st APRIL 1987

Shortly before he was due to join Nottinghamshire for his final season of county cricket, New Zealand's Richard Hadlee achieved his highest Test score. With the contest against Sri Lanka, in Colombo, drifting towards a draw after many rain interruptions, Hadlee batted throughout the final day to post a score of 151 not out, sharing in an unbroken stand of 246 with his captain Jeff Crowe, who made 120 not out.

THURSDAY 22nd APRIL 1971

Preparing for the new season, Nottinghamshire almost slipped to an embarrassing defeat in a friendly against Lincolnshire at the Carlton Forum. In a 40-over match, the first-class county only made an all-out score of 137. The Lincs side, including former Notts men Ian Moore and Mervyn Winfield, appeared on course for a shock victory until three wickets for Mike Taylor halted their progress and they fell 22 runs short.

WEDNESDAY 23rd APRIL 2003

South African Test player Steve Elworthy was enlisted as Nottinghamshire's overseas recruit for the early part of the 2003 campaign. His best bowling performance came in a drawn championship match against Lancashire at Old Trafford when he recorded figures of 5-71.

SATURDAY 24th APRIL 1965

Born in Newark, Paul Johnson is Nottinghamshire's tenth-highest first-class run scorer of all time. In a career that spanned from 1982 until 2002, the right-hander amassed 20,534 runs for the county, at an average of 36.40. The largest of his 40 centuries was the 187 he scored against Lancashire at Old Trafford in 1993. Johnson also played a further 383 one-day matches, scoring 10,025 runs at 31.82.

FRIDAY 24th APRIL 1998

After an opening day wash-out, Somerset's championship match at Taunton against Nottinghamshire began late but provided a career high for Mark Bowen. The Notts seam bowler claimed the first six wickets to fall and eventually finished with figures of 7-73, the best return of his 67-match first-class career. More wet weather brought a swift and unsatisfactory conclusion to the eventual outcome though.

THURSDAY 25th APRIL 2002

South Africa's Lance Klusener earned a deserved reputation for hard-hitting and quick scoring. Sadly, those qualities weren't allowed to shine on his first championship appearance for Nottinghamshire, as he was clean bowled by Middlesex's Simon Cook for a seven-ball 0 at Lord's. Klusener did make 42 in the second innings – and took 1-88 with the ball, although it was his only first-class appearance during a short-term registration.

FRIDAY 26th APRIL 1963

Bowlers are generally told to bowl straight so that "if they miss you hit". In a pre-season friendly at Trent Bridge, against Nottingham University, Andrew Corran's medium-pace bowling proved too slippery for the students to handle. He took 7-21 from 17 overs, hitting the stumps on six occasions.

SATURDAY 26th APRIL 2003

Stephen Fleming scored ten first-class centuries for Nottinghamshire, one more than in Tests for New Zealand. None of his county scores could match the magnificent career-high 274 not out he scored when leading his country against Sri Lanka in Colombo. For good measure, he added an unbeaten 69 in the second innings of the drawn contest.

SATURDAY 27th APRIL 1968

The first Nottinghamshire wicketkeeper to take five catches in a List A fixture was Deryck Murray. Against Lancashire at Trent Bridge, he caught Graham Atkinson, Jack Bond, John Sullivan, Ken Shuttleworth and Peter Lever in a winning Gillette Cup match. Murray repeated the feat a year later in the same competition, against Yorkshire at Scarborough. Only Chris Read has since emulated Murray's achievements.

SUNDAY 27th APRIL 1969

The opening round of the very first John Player League competition saw Nottinghamshire travel to Chelmsford to face Essex. The home side made 185-9 with Notts only able to muster 148 all out in reply.

FRIDAY 27th APRIL 2001

The highest score by a Nottinghamshire player on debut for the county is the 133 scored by the Australian batsman Greg Blewett against Durham at Trent Bridge.

FRIDAY 27th APRIL 2007

Passing his previous highest score by three runs, Samit Patel's 176 helped Nottinghamshire to a championship win over Gloucestershire at Bristol. He faced 203 balls and batted for 233 minutes, hitting 28 fours and three sixes.

THURSDAY 28th APRIL 1994

West Indian Test player Jimmy Adams began his Nottinghamshire career on a high note, scoring 117 on his first-class debut for the county, against Oxford University at The Parks. He added an unbeaten 52 in the second innings and went on to score 950 runs from 18 games during his only season at Trent Bridge. David Pipes, aged just 17 years and two days, made his only appearance for Notts in the same match and was dismissed by Chris Hollins – later to become better known as a BBC sports journalist and winner of *Strictly Come Dancing* in 2009.

FRIDAY 28th APRIL 2000

Making up for lost time after the opening two days of the match had been lost to the elements, Nottinghamshire and Northamptonshire gave a small crowd value for money – although not by the quality of their batting. Nineteen wickets fell on a day that saw the ECB pitch liaison officer summoned. Northants made 153, seamer David Millns taking 5-58, his best performance in Nottinghamshire colours. The home side then limped to 79-9 by the close with Devon Malcolm taking five wickets of his own. Rain returned to rule out any play on the fourth day and no action was taken as a result of the surface.

WEDNESDAY 29th APRIL 1942

Anthony "Robin" Bilbie was born at Sherwood and made his first-class debut for Nottinghamshire in 1960, scoring 39 in his first innings – a score that would remain his highest throughout the 14 matches he appeared in. A right-handed batsman, he only scored 291 in total for the county at an average of 11.19.

SUNDAY 30th APRIL 1905

The scorer of the highest individual figure for Nottinghamshire was born in Shirebrook in Derbyshire. William Walter Keeton's first-class career spanned from 1926 until 1952, with the highlight being his two Test match appearances for England. He completed the full-house of scoring a century against every other first-class county, with his 312 not out, against Middlesex at The Oval in 1939, surpassing everything that all other Notts batsmen have produced. Keeton also played professional football for Nottingham Forest and Sunderland. He died in Forest Town in October 1980.

NOTTINGHAMSHIRE CCC
On This Day

MAY

MONDAY 1st MAY 1944

David Anthony Pullan kept wicket for Nottinghamshire between 1970 and 1974. Born in Farsley, Yorkshire, he played 95 first-class matches, claiming 234 dismissals, of which 27 were stumpings. He also played 49 List A fixtures, which produced a further 45 victims. A right-handed batsman, his top score for the county was 34, made against Warwickshire in 1972.

SATURDAY 1st MAY 1965

Having been knocked out in the first round in the previous two seasons Nottinghamshire won their first Gillette Cup match at the third time of asking. Playing at Trent Bridge they defeated Wiltshire by seven wickets with Andrew Corran's 4-35 earning him the man of the match award.

WEDNESDAY 2nd MAY 1962

Nottinghamshire's first-ever competitive one-day match saw them defeated by Northamptonshire at Trent Bridge. In a low scoring contest the visitors posted 168-9, with John Cotton taking 4-24. In reply, Notts could only make 137 all out, with skipper Geoff Millman making 60, the only half-century of the clash. The two sides, along with Leicestershire and Derbyshire, were pioneering a Midlands Knock-Out competition, played over 65 overs and Northants went on to defeat Leicestershire in the final.

SUNDAY 2nd MAY 1993

A tense and thrilling four-day match at Trent Bridge ended in the most dramatic of conclusions. Chasing 296 for victory over Worcestershire, last pair Mike Field-Buss and Andy Afford came together with Nottinghamshire needing six runs to win. They mustered five of them before Stuart Lampitt trapped Field-Buss in front, to bring about the only tied championship match that Notts have ever played in.

MONDAY 3rd MAY 1869

Wilford-born Alick Handford was a right-arm medium-pace bowler who took 43 wickets for Nottinghamshire between 1894 and 1898. His best of 7-75 came against Middlesex at Trent Bridge in 1894. Somewhat unusually, he had made his official first-class debut in a match in Philadelphia, USA in 1892, playing for the Players of the United States of America.

SUNDAY 3rd MAY 2009

Nottinghamshire achieved their highest-ever List A score, 346-9 against Ireland at Trent Bridge. Alex Hales scored 106, his first century for the county, Alistair Brown added 89 and Will Jefferson made 57 not out. Ireland replied with 212-9, losing the Friends Provident Trophy 50-over contest by 134 runs.

WEDNESDAY 3rd MAY 2006

The high spot of David Alleyne's 17 first-class matches for Nottinghamshire came in a championship game against Warwickshire at Trent Bridge. The wicketkeeper/batsman became the ninth player for the county to take nine or more dismissals in a match, claiming seven catches and two stumpings. To put even more gloss on his performance, Alleyne scored an undefeated 109 in Notts' first innings – the only century of his career.

THURSDAY 4th MAY 1978

Guy Edward Welton was born in Grimsby, Lincolnshire. A talented footballer, he was a youth trainee at his local club Grimsby Town but cricket took precedence and he made his championship and List A debuts for Nottinghamshire in 1997. A right-handed opening batsman, Welton scored 3,299 first-class runs at an average of 25.77 in 73 matches for Notts and a further 1,132 runs at 21.35 in one-day cricket.

THURSDAY 5th MAY 1966

Four years after retiring from first-class cricket, Roy Swetman returned to the game to play for Nottinghamshire. The former Surrey and 11-time capped England wicketkeeper made scores of 15 and 8 not out in a rain-ruined match against Kent at Trent Bridge. Swetman spent only two seasons with Notts but played 56 first-class matches for them, scoring 1,475 runs and claiming 107 catches and three stumpings.

SUNDAY 5th MAY 1996

Notts could thank Paul Pollard, who made 118 from 108 balls, and Paul Johnson's undefeated 97 from 78 for reaching 292-2 in the AXA Equity and Law League, against Sussex at Trent Bridge. The total was a new high for the county in the 40-over format and secured victory by 129 runs.

WEDNESDAY 6th MAY 1931

Harold Larwood and Bill Voce each produced fine individual performances as Nottinghamshire condemned Glamorgan to a 301-run defeat at Trent Bridge. After scoring 74 in the first innings, Larwood then took a hat-trick, dismissing Dai Davies, Trevor Every and Emrys Davies. His new-ball partner also showed he was no slouch with the bat, scoring 129 in the second innings, reaching his century in just 45 minutes – the quickest ever by a Notts player, with regards to time taken.

FRIDAY 6th MAY 1932

John David "Jack" Bond had been pivotal in helping Lancashire to win two John Player League titles and three Gillette Cup finals during his time at Old Trafford. Born at Kearsley, near Bolton, Bond looked to have called time on his career when he announced his retirement in 1972 but two years later he returned to the game as Nottinghamshire's player-manager. Unable to find the same level of success at Trent Bridge, he skippered the side for just one season, playing 17 first-class games which only produced 245 runs at an average of 12.25.

THURSDAY 6th MAY 2010

Steven Mullaney joined the exclusive list of Nottinghamshire batsmen who have scored a century on their first appearance for the county. Seventy-two not out overnight, the 23-year-old right-hander, who had joined the county from Lancashire during the previous winter, advanced to an unbeaten century against Hampshire at The Rose Bowl, Southampton.

FRIDAY 6th MAY 2011

At 291-8 Nottinghamshire were still 94 runs away from saving the follow-on in a championship match against Yorkshire at Trent Bridge. Batsmen Ben Phillips, on his county debut, and Andre Adams decided that if they were going down, then they were going down fighting. When they were parted, just 16.4 overs later, the pair had clubbed 114 for the ninth wicket in one of the most destructive displays of clean hitting ever seen on the ground. With each man clearing the ropes on three occasions, they took Notts to safety before Adams eventually fell for 54 (from 47 balls), leaving Phillips unbeaten on 70.

SATURDAY 7th MAY 2005

Nottinghamshire bettered any score they had ever achieved away from Trent Bridge when they visited Surrey at The Oval and made 692-7 declared. Captain Stephen Fleming scored 238 not out, Jason Gallian made 141 and former Surrey batsman Darren Bicknell added 91 against his old county. The total was surpassed with the county's fourth-highest of all time two years later when 791 was scored against Essex at Chelmsford.

FRIDAY 8th MAY 1914

There are few things in cricket as exciting as a new, young quick bowler making an early impression. Nottinghamshire's Fred Barratt certainly did that on his debut for the county. Playing against MCC at Lord's the raw 20-year-old returned figures of 8-91. Proving it was no fluke, he took 5-58 against Sussex a week later on his maiden championship appearance.

MONDAY 9th MAY 1921

Thomas Hugh Collins only made four first-class appearances but he left his mark in the record books by claiming a wicket with his first delivery for Nottinghamshire, the second bowler to do so. Playing against Leicestershire at Trent Bridge the slow left-arm spinner clean bowled John King, a 50-year-old former Test batsman.

WEDNESDAY 10th MAY 1916

Alexander Basil Crawford was killed in action at La Ventie, France, during the Great War. Born in Coleshill, he made 11 appearances for Nottinghamshire before the conflict. After becoming a Captain in the West Yorkshire Regiment he set sail for France in January 1916. The Divisional History for this day recorded: "A few quiet days followed, during which Captain AB Crawford and Captain GS de Williams were unfortunately killed in the lion by shell burst." Crawford died aged 24 and was buried at St Vaast Post Military Cemetery.

TUESDAY 10th MAY 2011

A day on which Nottinghamshire's Andre Adams had a milestone to celebrate. Playing against Sussex at Hove, the New Zealand-born swing bowler dismissed Monty Panesar to collect the 500th wicket of his career.

TUESDAY 11th MAY 1993

Nottinghamshire came out second best in a thrilling Benson and Hedges Cup match against Somerset at Trent Bridge. Notts had posted 279-6 and reduced their opponents to 278-9 in the final over. Debutant Andre van Troost, a tall Dutch fast bowler, hit Chris Cairns away for a boundary off the final ball of the match to seal a one-wicket victory for the Cidermen.

TUESDAY 12th MAY 1964

John Andrew "Andy" Afford, a slow left-arm bowler who played for Nottinghamshire between 1984 and 1997, was born in Crowland, Lincolnshire. In 168 first-class matches for the county, he took 464 wickets at an average of 32.97, with a best of 6-51 against Lancashire. He took more than 50 wickets in a season on five separate occasions, with a best of 57 in 1991. Afford was a member of the 1987 championship-winning side and he also played in 50 one-day matches for the county, picking up a further 46 wickets.

WEDNESDAY 12th MAY 1971

Mike Harris scored 118 in the first innings of Nottinghamshire's match at Grace Road against Leicestershire and followed it up with 123 in the second innings. During the course of the 1971 season the opener registered seven more centuries – the equal most in a year by any player for the county. He totalled 2,238 runs at an average of 50.86.

TUESDAY 12th MAY 1987

There have been few collapses to rival Nottinghamshire's in a Benson and Hedges Cup match against Leicestershire at Grace Road. Starting brightly, Mick Newell and Tim Robinson put on 43 for the first wicket. What happened next defies belief. Their demise wasn't totally self-induced, with West Indian quick bowler Winston Benjamin hurrying them to an ignominious total by collecting four wickets in six balls, including a hat-trick with the wickets of Paul Johnson, Richard Hadlee and Bruce French. At 62-6 play was abandoned for the day but the following morning Benjamin took another wicket to claim 5-26 with Notts all out for just 74. They had lost all ten wickets for just 31 runs with the five batsmen between three and seven in the order all recording ducks.

FRIDAY 13th MAY 1898

Arthur Bradley Wheat was a devoted servant to Nottinghamshire County Cricket Club, playing for more than a decade and then serving as first-team scorer from 1947 until his death in 1973. Born in Halam, he played semi-professional football for Sutton Town and Alfreton Town and joined the Notts staff as a wicketkeeper in 1923 but had to wait four years for his debut. He made 91 appearances, claiming 174 dismissals.

FRIDAY 13th MAY 1983

Many cricketers have failed to give a good account of themselves when on trial at counties. That criticism can't be levelled at Robbie Kerr, Queensland's 22-year-old right-handed batsman. Opening a seven-match stint with Notts' seconds, he scored 125 against Warwickshire, on his way to a total of 824 runs and an average of 82.4. Amongst his four scores over 100 were contributions of 202 not out and 102, in the same match against Derbyshire at Heanor. With Richard Hadlee and Clive Rice occupying the overseas spots at Trent Bridge, Kerr had to look elsewhere for fame and fortune but did go on to make two Test and four one-day appearances for Australia.

WEDNESDAY 14th MAY 1980

One-day best figures of 4-17 by Lancashire's David Lloyd condemned Nottinghamshire to defeat in a Benson and Hedges Cup group match at Old Trafford. The significance of the result meant that it was the Red Rose county who secured home advantage in the quarter-finals, with Notts having to travel to Northants – where they lost.

THURSDAY 15th MAY 1890

Nottinghamshire certainly had the better of things on the opening day of their championship match against Sussex at Trent Bridge. At stumps they had reached 341-1, with Arthur Shrewsbury unbeaten on 164 and Billy Gunn on 152. The pair had come together with the score on 26 when John Dixon was dismissed and extended their stand to an eventual 398, the highest second-wicket stand for the county. Gunn was eventually dismissed for 196, while Shrewsbury went on to make 267 – bizarrely equalling his career-high total made against Middlesex three years earlier.

SUNDAY 16th MAY 1976

Twenty20 specialist Dirk Peter Nannes was born in Victoria, Australia, but represented the Netherlands, as well as the country of his birth, before joining Nottinghamshire for the 2010 English domestic competition. In a campaign eventually stifled at the semi-final stage, the left-arm quick bowler played 16 times for the Outlaws, taking 17 wickets at an average of 27.41.

SATURDAY 16th MAY 2009

Samit Patel's first six-wicket haul in List A competition for Nottinghamshire came in the Friends Provident Trophy. Against Ireland at Castle Avenue, Dublin, the slow left-arm spinner took 6-13 to secure the man of the match prize.

SUNDAY 16th MAY 2010

Nottinghamshire were well represented as England lifted the ICC World Twenty20 title with victory over Australia in Barbados. Stuart Broad, Ryan Sidebottom and Graeme Swann were members of the victorious side, whilst David Hussey and Dirk Nannes – due to join Notts a month later – were in the defeated 11. Additionally, there were further connections, with Kevin Pietersen, an ex-Notts player, and Michael Lumb, who joined the county ahead of the 2012 season. The official presentation party after the final included Sir Garfield Sobers, himself a Nottinghamshire legend.

FRIDAY 17th MAY 1895

For the first time Nottinghamshire passed 700 in a single innings. Billy Gunn's 219, plus centuries from Richard Howitt, who made 119, and Robert Bagguley, 110, helped produce a total of 726 at Trent Bridge against Sussex. Dismissing their opponents for 170, and then 178, ensured a win by an innings and 378 runs, which remains the highest margin ever inflicted by Notts.

MONDAY 17th MAY 1948

A record crowd of 35,000 flocked in to Trent Bridge on Bank Holiday Monday, the second day of a match between Notts and Surrey. They saw centuries from Joe Hardstaff junior and Walter Keeton move the home side to a total of 420-9 declared, a first innings lead of just one. A day later the pair combined again to seal a thrilling four-wicket victory.

SATURDAY 18th MAY 2002

The new Trent Bridge library, located in the reception and squash court complex at the back of the pavilion, was officially opened by the Rt Hon Kenneth Clarke, QC, MP, the president of Nottinghamshire County Cricket Club. Containing more than 15,000 cricket books, it is the second largest in the UK, with only the library at Lord's containing more.

FRIDAY 19th MAY 1972

During a professional career from 1959 to 1976 Barry Stead played 232 first-class matches for Yorkshire, Essex, MCC, Northern Transvaal and Nottinghamshire, where he spent the bulk of his career. The left-arm quick bowler took 653 first-class wickets, with a best of 8-44 which came on this day, at Trent Bridge against Somerset, and included a hat-trick of Roy Virgin, Richard Cooper and Brian Close.

MONDAY 19th MAY 1975

Nottinghamshire made short work of a Benson and Hedges Cup match at Elm Avenue, Newark. Minor Counties North were bowled out for just 67, with Notts then wrapping up a comfortable seven-wicket victory. Top-scorer for the MCN was the England and British Lions rugby union fly-half Alan Old, brother of Yorkshire and England fast bowler Chris Old. Following his 19 with the bat, Alan then returned impressive figures of 11-4-13-1.

SATURDAY 20th MAY 1911

Ted Alletson produced a display of hitting rarely seen, either before or since, to avert an inevitable defeat against Sussex at Hove. Coming in to bat at number nine, with his side only nine runs ahead with just three wickets left, he scored 47 in 50 minutes before lunch and was then told to "have a go" by captain Arthur Jones. Alletson's response was to blast a further 142 in the next 40 minutes. At one point he scored 115 out of 120 in just seven overs. His onslaught included one over (which included two no-balls) from Ernest Killick, a slow left-armer, which went for 34 runs – four fours and three sixes – a record that stood until 1968 when another Nottinghamshire batsman, Garfield Sobers, surpassed it.

THURSDAY 20th MAY 1943

Former West Indies wicketkeeper Deryck Lance Murray was born in Port-of-Spain, Trinidad. He made five Test appearances in 1963 before coming to England to study and his educational commitments enabled him to qualify to play county cricket so he joined Nottinghamshire during 1966, making his debut against Yorkshire at Bramall Lane, Sheffield. A more than capable right-handed batsman and wicketkeeper, Murray played 97 first-class matches for Nottinghamshire, scoring 3,873 runs and claiming 172 dismissals. In his sixth appearance in county cricket he made the highest score of his career, 166 not out, against Surrey at The Oval. Murray later went on to appear in 62 Tests as well as playing in the West Indies' World Cup-winning sides of 1975 and 1979.

SATURDAY 21st MAY 1927

The Rev William Bury was born in Radcliffe-on-Trent in 1839 and was educated privately at Trinity College, Cambridge, where he was awarded his Blue in 1861 and 1862. One of eight brothers, he played three matches for Notts but only excelled in the field, earning the nickname of "Deerfoot" for the speed of his running. He scored two centuries at Trent Bridge – both ending on 121, for the Gentlemen of North v South and the other for Midland County Diamonds v Free Foresters. Bury later appeared for Northants, having become a vicar in Hazelbeach. He died on this day in Borough Green, near Sevenoaks.

MONDAY 22nd MAY 1826

George Parr was born in Radcliffe-on-Trent and will forever hold his place in the Nottinghamshire annals as their first century-maker in a county match, scoring 130 against Surrey in 1859. Parr played 53 matches for Notts without ever reaching three figures again. The right-handed batsman scored a total of 1,770 runs, adding to a further 4,856 he made whilst representing other sides, including the All England Eleven. He skippered Notts and also captained the first England touring side to travel overseas, leading them in North America. His favourite sweep shot often landed in the elm trees on the Bridgford Road side of the Trent Bridge ground, where a stand was named in his honour, until replaced by The New Stand in 2008. Parr died in 1891, aged 65.

MIKE HARRIS — 9 CENTURIES FOR NOTTS IN 1971

WEDNESDAY 22nd MAY 1963

One-day knock-out cricket was introduced in 1963 with the advent of the Gillette Cup, originally played at 65 overs per side. Nottinghamshire's first match ended in a four-wicket defeat against Yorkshire at Acklam Park, Middlesbrough. Brian Bolus, playing against the county he left a few months earlier, opened the batting and scored an undefeated 100 in Notts' disappointing 159 all out, with Fred Trueman collecting four cheap wickets for the home side.

FRIDAY 23rd MAY 1930

The final day of Nottinghamshire's match against Hampshire at Southampton was never going to give much value for the admission price as the home side needed just one more run for victory. Notts took to the field in lounge suits, rather than in traditional whites, Fred Barratt and Bill Voce even wearing their overcoats. The second delivery, bowled by Arthur Carr, was hit away for four by Alex Kennedy, enabling the visitors to make a speedy getaway for their long journey home.

TUESDAY 23rd MAY 1978

Gareth David Clough was born in Leeds and after beginning his career with his home county he moved to Trent Bridge in 2001. A lively, right-arm medium-pace bowler, he bagged 16 wickets in 11 four-day fixtures for Notts. Clough took another 86 wickets in 96 limited-overs appearances and collected 31 wickets from 39 Twenty20 matches. He was a member of the defeated Outlaws side that played in the 2006 final.

SUNDAY 23rd MAY 1993.

On the occasion that Nottinghamshire wore their green one-day clothing for the first time, they defeated Kent by nine wickets at Trent Bridge in the AXA Equity and Law League. With 6-52, Chris Cairns' best one-day bowling figures for Notts had restricted the visitors to 264-9 from their allotted 50 overs. The victory chase was successfully completed in just 35.2 overs thanks to Paul Johnson's unbeaten 167 – the highest individual one-day score by a Nottinghamshire batsman. Johnson and Tim Robinson shared in an unbroken second-wicket stand of 213, the highest for any wicket in List A cricket for the county.

MONDAY 24th MAY 1993

After their one-day victory over Kent the previous day, Nottinghamshire completed a championship win over the same side and re-wrote the record books in the process. For the first time since 1863 the county won a match after being asked to follow on. Trailing by 152 runs, they made 330 in their second innings and then dismissed their opponents for 104, with Mike Field-Buss taking 6-42 and Andy Afford grabbing 4-35.

THURSDAY 24th MAY 2007

David Hussey made the fourth-highest individual score by a Nottinghamshire batsman on the second day of a championship match against Essex at Trent Bridge. The Australian hit 27 fours and 14 sixes in a 280-minute innings of 275. He faced 227 balls and shared in a county-record fifth-wicket stand of 359 in 54 overs with Chris Read, who scored 165. Notts declared after reaching a total of 664-7 and bowled out their opposition to win by an innings.

THURSDAY 25th MAY 1944

Michael John Harris was born in St Just-in-Roseland, Cornwall and began his career with Middlesex. Moving to Nottinghamshire ahead of the 1969 season, the right-handed opening batsman (and occasional wicketkeeper) was one of the most consistent and reliable performers for the county over a 14-year stretch. With 15,308 runs at 38.46 he was considered unlucky not to gain international selection, particularly during 1971 when he plundered 2,238 runs, with nine centuries – a feat only equalled by "Dodger" Whysall and Chris Broad in Notts colours.

SATURDAY 25th MAY 1957

Garfield Sobers batted 71 times at Trent Bridge in first-class cricket but his highest score came on his maiden appearance. Opening the batting for the West Indies in a tour match against Nottinghamshire, he stroked his way to an elegant 219 not out, sharing in a second-wicket stand of 193 with Clyde Walcott, who hit 115. Showing just how cricket's fortunes can change, Sobers made a second-innings duck, bowled by Arthur Jepson. Sobers' only wicket in the drawn match was that of Bruce Dooland, caught behind by Rohan Kanhai.

TUESDAY 25th MAY 1982

Clive Rice scored seven centuries in his 274 List A appearances for Nottinghamshire. His highest score was the unbeaten 130 he made in the 93-run Benson and Hedges Cup win over Scotland at Glasgow.

FRIDAY 25th MAY 1990

Set 341 from a minimum of 70 overs against Northants at Trent Bridge, Nottinghamshire completed one of their most convincing chases of all time. From 95-2 just before tea, Paul Johnson and Duncan Martindale went on the attack. Johnson rattled up a century from 88 deliveries and went on to an undefeated 165 from 120, with 24 fours and a six. At the other end Duncan Martindale scored 108, the pair sharing 249 in just 35 overs to complete an extraordinary victory with 5.2 overs and eight wickets to spare.

TUESDAY 26th MAY 1903

Nottinghamshire's highest first-class score at Trent Bridge was achieved against Leicestershire and was compiled in just 167 overs. In a total of 739-7 declared, three batsmen passed 100, with a fourth, James Iremonger, making 94. John Gunn made 294, adding a county record 367 for the third wicket with his uncle, Billy Gunn, who scored 139. The declaration came just after John Dixon had also passed three figures and he ended with an unbeaten 104. Although Leicestershire were made to follow on, they did bat out for a draw in their second innings.

MONDAY 27th MAY 1861

John Auger Dixon captained Nottinghamshire for a decade at the end of the 19th century. As a right-handed batsman his highest first-class score of 268 not out, against Sussex, broke the county record and he declared the innings closed once he had passed Arthur Shrewsbury's previous best of 267. He led the team in 1889 when they shared the county title with Surrey and Lancashire and the following year he skippered the county to an innings victory over the touring Australians. Born in Grantham, he died at The Park in Nottingham in 1931 and the main gates at Trent Bridge were erected in his memory two years later.

MONDAY 27th MAY 1935

Bob Winrow only played in seven first-class matches for Nottinghamshire, yet he managed to write his name into the county record books. Batting at number nine in the order, he scored his only century, 137 versus Somerset at Trent Bridge. In so doing he played his part in a record eighth-wicket stand of 220 with his skipper, George Heane, who made 101.

WEDNESDAY 27th MAY 1964

Maurice Hill played in 20 List A matches for Nottinghamshire, scoring 334 runs, with one century. His 107 against Somerset at Taunton helped his side to an all-out total of 215 in a second round Gillette Cup match and won him the man of the match award. Unfortunately, the home side managed to tie the scores at 215-9 and won by virtue of losing fewer wickets.

MONDAY 27th MAY 1974

With 140 of his runs coming in boundaries, Hampshire's Barry Richards carried his bat in scoring an unbeaten 225 out of his side's all-out total of 344. The South African's fluency was almost enough to defeat Nottinghamshire on his own at Trent Bridge, with the home side falling for just 98 and 145, to lose by an innings and 101 runs.

SATURDAY 27th MAY 1989

Trent Bridge witnessed the closest possible finish as a one-day international between England and Australia ended in a tie. Allan Lamb scored an undefeated 100 as England posted 226-5 from their 55 overs, with the Australians matching that score, ending their innings on 226-8.

THURSDAY 27th MAY 1999

Nottinghamshire were dismissed for 324 on the first day of their PPP Healthcare County Championship match against Hampshire at Trent Bridge. Nothing particularly unusual about that – except the top scorer in the innings was extras with 73. Made up of 25 byes, 18 leg-byes, six no-balls and 24 wides, the contribution was the most ever recorded in a single innings against Notts.

SATURDAY 28th MAY 1921

Thomas Leonard "Tich" Richmond made his only Test appearance for England on his home ground, Trent Bridge, against Australia. Amidst the pomp and ceremony of the 100th Test between the two nations, the Nottinghamshire leg-break and googly bowler returned match figures of 2-86 and was considered unlucky not to be selected again.

FRIDAY 29th MAY 2009

An explosive innings of 90 not out from Graeme Swann took Notts Outlaws to a comfortable eight-wicket Twenty20 win over Derbyshire at the County Ground. The home side had posted 158-5 but the total was rendered insufficient by a 47-ball blitz from the England off-spinner. Swann's knock included 13 fours and two sixes as his side sped to success with 29 deliveries still remaining.

TUESDAY 30th MAY 1905

Archie Maclaren scored the first Test century at Trent Bridge. Batting in a side which included two Nottinghamshire players, Arthur Jones and John Gunn, the Lancashire opener made a score of 140. England were later spun to victory by an 8-107 second innings performance from Bernard Bosanquet, the acclaimed inventor of the googly.

SUNDAY 30th MAY 1976

It always pays to check with the umpires! Needing four to win a John Player League match at Lord's, Middlesex's Mike Gatting thought he'd hit the required boundary and walked towards the pavilion in celebration. A smart stop and throw from Nottinghamshire's Barry Stead brought about one of the easiest – and most controversial – run-outs ever seen at the Home of Cricket. Gatting's 85 wasn't in vain as his team-mates clinched the victory in the next over.

FRIDAY 31st MAY 1974

Elm Avenue, Newark, was the venue for Derek Randall's Nottinghamshire debut. Playing in the championship against Essex, he scored 78 in his only innings of the draw. The 21-year-old from Retford arrived at 92-5 and made his runs in 140 minutes, hitting four boundaries and five sixes.

NOTTINGHAMSHIRE CCC
On This Day

JUNE

THURSDAY 1st JUNE 1899

Trent Bridge staged its first Test, with Billy Gunn the Nottinghamshire representative in the England line-up against Australia. Gunn made scores of 14 and 3 in the drawn contest, which saw Dr WG Grace play his final Test, aged 50 years 320 days at its conclusion. Only Wilfred Rhodes played for England at a greater age, and by coincidence, he made his debut in this match.

FRIDAY 1st JUNE 2001

No-one has scored more on his Nottinghamshire debut than the Australian batsman Greg Blewett, who hit an undefeated 137 against Durham at Chester-le-Street in his first innings for the county.

MONDAY 2nd JUNE 1947

Michael Kenneth Bore took 162 first-class wickets for Yorkshire before joining Nottinghamshire in 1979. Originally a left-arm medium-pacer, before reverting to slow left-arm after his switch to Trent Bridge, he enjoyed a productive spell with his second county. In 85 matches he took 210 wickets at 30.36 with a best of 8-89. Born in East Hull, Bore also played 92 List A matches for Notts, taking 89 wickets at 28.95, with a best of 6-22 against Leicestershire in 1980.

SATURDAY 2nd JUNE 1990

Chris Broad scored exactly 50 centuries during his 340-match first-class career. The highest came whilst representing Nottinghamshire against Kent at the Nevill Ground, Tunbridge Wells. The left-hander scored 227 not out, sharing a fourth-wicket stand of 285 with Derek Randall, who scored 178. Notts declared their first innings on 477-6 and enforced the follow-on but weren't able to convert their advantage into a victory.

SATURDAY 3rd JUNE 1893

The third morning of Nottinghamshire's match against Somerset at Trent Bridge saw fast bowler Frank Shacklock re-write the county records. Dismissing Spurway, Gibbs and Newton in Somerset's second innings, he became the fifth man to take a hat-trick for Notts. The next ball though, he went one better, making it four in four by removing Trask. All four Somerset batsmen had been dismissed the same way – clean bowled.

THURSDAY 3rd JUNE 1976

Trent Bridge hosted the opening Test between England and the West Indies. With Vivian Richards scoring an outstanding 232, the visitors had the better of the draw, whilst the comments of England captain Tony Greig, who vowed to "make the West Indies grovel", rebounded on him somewhat as he was dismissed for 0 by Andy Roberts.

TUESDAY 4th JUNE 1968

Nottinghamshire's bowlers were made to toil as two of Warwickshire's stars made the most of batsman-friendly conditions. West Indian Test player Rohan Kanhai scored 253, with Pakistan's Khalid Ibadulla unbeaten on 147. They combined to add 402 for the fourth wicket, the highest partnership for any wicket against Notts.

SUNDAY 4th JUNE 1972

Fittingly, Garfield Sobers turned on the style in his own benefit match at Trent Bridge. The West Indian scoring a hard-hitting 96 not out, containing three sixes and nine fours, in the John Player League against Surrey. Although a crowd of 4,000 realised £481 for the beneficiary, the day ended in disappointment for the Nottinghamshire captain as the visitors reached their target of 158 in the penultimate over.

WEDNESDAY 4th JUNE 1975

Medium-fast bowler Alex Wharf was born in Bradford and played for Yorkshire before joining Nottinghamshire for two seasons in the late 1990s. Whilst at Trent Bridge he took 40 wickets and scored two half-centuries in his 21 first-class matches. List A cricket saw him collect 16 wickets from 23 games. Later, after moving to Glamorgan, he gained England recognition and appeared in 13 ODIs.

SATURDAY 4th JUNE 1983

Mike Hendrick took 100 first-class wickets for Nottinghamshire, at an average of just 16.81. His best figures came at Trent Bridge against Leicestershire, who were dismissed for just 101 in 39.3 overs. Hendrick's full analysis was 15.3-4-17-6. The match took a dramatic twist later as the visitors rallied to earn a draw. In the final session, set 159 to win, Notts slumped to 32-8 with time up.

SUNDAY 4th JUNE 2000

A combination of youth and experience produced Nottinghamshire's highest first-wicket partnership. Guy Welton, 22, partnered by Darren Bicknell, ten years older, put on an unbroken 406 against Warwickshire at Edgbaston. Welton had not advanced beyond 95 in the championship before but went on to turn his first century into an undefeated 200, whilst his partner ended on 180 not out in the draw.

SUNDAY 5th JUNE 1966

Nottinghamshire's first championship match to include Sunday play also produced one of the most bizarre endings. Chasing 238 on the final day, Hampshire were 236-5 with one ball remaining. Henry Horton played the ball forward and set off for the run but appeared to deliberately kick the ball away from the fielders as he completed the single. Reports indicated it was a clear case of obstructing the field. After half an hour of deliberations, Notts captain Brian Bolus confirmed that his side had not made an appeal for such a dismissal. Hampshire, having ended the match with the scores level, were thereby awarded five extra points. Sunday's play – day two of the match – saw spectators admitted to the ground without charge provided a scorecard was bought at the increased price of one shilling.

THURSDAY 5th JUNE 1975

Nottinghamshire had an unfamiliar top scorer in their side when they faced the West Indies in a 50-over match at Trent Bridge. With the fixture used as a warm-up ahead of the impending ICC World Cup, Jamaica's Maurice Foster was loaned to Notts for the day to get some useful match practice against his regular team-mates. Chasing a score of 234-6, which included 50s from Rohan Kanhai and Alvin Kallicharran, Notts fell 33 short with Foster run out for 58.

THURSDAY 5th JUNE 2008

The New Stand, on the Bridgford Road side of the Trent Bridge ground, was officially opened by HRH The Duke of Edinburgh. The single-tier construction replaced the Parr Stand which had been demolished at the end of the previous season.

FRIDAY 5th JUNE 2009

There was last-over disappointment for Nottinghamshire's Stuart Broad as England slipped to a shock four-wicket defeat to Holland in the opening match of the ICC World Twenty20 at Lord's. With seven required from the last over – and two from the last ball – Broad was unable to stop Ryan ten Doeschate and Edgar Schiferli seeing the minnows through to a historic victory, the winning run coming from an overthrow.

SUNDAY 5th JUNE 2011

In the ninth year of the domestic Twenty20 competition the Notts Outlaws posted their highest total by scoring 215-6 against Yorkshire at Trent Bridge. Adam Voges, with 74, and Samit Patel, who made 52, scored the bulk of the runs against Yorkshire, who could only make 162-8 in reply.

THURSDAY 6th JUNE 1963

Wicketkeeper Deryck Murray made his Test debut for the West Indies against England at Old Trafford. Three years before he first played for Nottinghamshire, the Trinidadian held six catches during the match, as well as making seven not out during his side's ten-wicket success.

MONDAY 6th JUNE 1994

Brian Lara took cricket's highest-ever score to a new level for Warwickshire against Durham, at Edgbaston. Surpassing the 499 set by Hanif Mohammad in 1959, he reached a new landmark – 501 not out – with a boundary off the bowling of John Morris. Later to move to Trent Bridge, Morris wasn't the only Nottinghamshire connection to this feat because wicketkeeper Chris Scott, who played 63 times for the county before joining Durham, spilled Lara when the Trinidadian batsman had only made 18.

SATURDAY 7th JUNE 1890

The first time a Nottinghamshire captain had declared an innings closed was against Kent at the Bat and Ball Ground in Gravesend. On the final day, skipper Charles Wright closed his side's second innings on 157-5, leaving Kent a target of 231. The bold tactic nearly paid off, Kent clinging on to draw at 98-9.

FRIDAY 7th JUNE 2002

Batting for MCC against Sri Lanka, Nottinghamshire's Usman Afzaal scored an undefeated 111, from 174 deliveries with 11 fours and three sixes. County colleague Chris Read scored 24, sharing 68 for the sixth wicket with Afzaal but rain had already disrupted much of the three-day fixture, forcing an inevitable draw at Queen's Park, Chesterfield.

MONDAY 8th JUNE 1925

Arthur Carr scored 43 centuries for Nottinghamshire between 1913 and 1934, the largest coming against Leicestershire at Aylestone Road, Leicester. His score of 206 helped his side to a victory by an innings and 155 runs. The match was also significant as it marked the end of Thomas Oates' career. Approaching his 50th birthday, the wicketkeeper bowed out having played 420 matches for Notts, capturing a record 967 dismissals (744 catches and 223 stumpings).

WEDNESDAY 8th JUNE 2011

Darren Pattinson became only the second Nottinghamshire bowler, after Richard Logan in 2003, to take five wickets in a domestic Twenty20 match when he did so in a North Group clash against Warwickshire at Edgbaston. His 5-25 helped his side to victory by 28 runs.

SATURDAY 9th JUNE 1951

An immensely proud day for all Nottinghamshire cricket-lovers as Reg Simpson scored a Test hundred on his home ground. Against South Africa at Trent Bridge, he batted for 270 minutes and stroked 21 boundaries in his 137. Sadly, there was to be no fairytale ending to the match, with the tourists winning by 71 runs.

THURSDAY 9th JUNE 1983

Trent Bridge staged one of the biggest shocks in World Cup history when Zimbabwe beat Australia by 13 runs. Nine years before they became a Test-playing nation, the minnows made 239-6 from their 60 overs and restricted Australia to 226-7. Duncan Fletcher, later to become head coach of both England and India, won the man of the match award for his 69 not out and 4-42 in the Zimbabwe victory.

FRIDAY 9th JUNE 2000

On his 23rd birthday Usman Afzaal became a joint-record holder for Nottinghamshire. Batting against Worcestershire at Trent Bridge he scored 151 not out, sharing in a stand of 152 for the final wicket with Andrew "AJ" Harris, who made 39. The partnership equalled that of EB Alletson and W Riley, against Sussex at Hove in 1911. Within sight of the outright record Harris hit his own wicket when facing the bowling of Worcestershire's Glenn McGrath, who returned figures of 8-86.

THURSDAY 10th JUNE 2004

One season before skippering Nottinghamshire to the County Championship, Stephen Fleming gained an affinity with Trent Bridge by scoring a Test century on the ground. The New Zealand left-hander, opening the batting, scored 117 on the first day of the third Test against England although his side eventually lost the match by four wickets.

WEDNESDAY 10th JUNE 2009

Trent Bridge staged the 100th Twenty20 international, with Sri Lanka defeating the West Indies by 15 runs. The fixture was one of ten held at the ground as part of the ICC World Twenty20, which was eventually won by Pakistan, who defeated Sri Lanka in the final at Lord's.

SATURDAY 11th JUNE 1921

John Gunn enjoyed a fine all-round performance as Nottinghamshire defeated Lancashire at Trent Bridge by 177 runs. Batting at number three, he made 148 in the first innings, before going on to collect a match haul of ten wickets, with figures of 8-80 and 2-31.

SATURDAY 11th JUNE 1927

William Attewell died in Long Eaton, one day before his 66th birthday. In 283 matches for Nottinghamshire the medium-pacer took 1,303 wickets, at 15.52, with a best of 9-23 against Sussex at Trent Bridge. No mean performer with the bat, he also made one first-class hundred, against Kent in 1897. As an all-rounder, he represented England in ten Test matches between 1884 and 1892, with nine of the matches taking place in Australia.

SUNDAY 11th JUNE 2000

Andrew "AJ" Harris claimed one five-wicket haul in List A cricket during his time at Nottinghamshire. Playing at Trent Bridge against Hampshire he took 5-35 in an eight-wicket victory.

SATURDAY 11th JUNE 1927

Nottinghamshire were the visitors when the BBC broadcast its first ball-by-ball commentary of a championship match, against Middlesex at Lord's. Listeners heard Pelham Warner's description of an opening day that saw Notts make 381, before the home side closed on 44-0. The remaining two days weren't covered but ended with a ten-wicket success for Nottinghamshire.

MONDAY 11th JUNE 1956

The only recorded instance of a Nottinghamshire bowler taking all ten opposition wickets in a championship match came at Erinold Park in Stroud when Ken Smales recorded figures of 41.3-20-66-10 in Gloucestershire's first-innings total of 214. Incredibly, despite the performance of the off-spinner, Notts went on to lose by nine wickets!

SUNDAY 11th JUNE 2006

Although their mighty effort still ended in defeat, Nottinghamshire's Chris Read and AJ Harris broke the world List A ninth-wicket record when they came together at 95-8, chasing 281 to win. Facing Durham, at Trent Bridge in the Cheltenham and Gloucester Trophy, both batsmen achieved career-high scores, Read making 135 and his partner scoring 34. Both were then dismissed in quick succession, after adding 155 in the 28-run loss.

SATURDAY 12th JUNE 1937

Between 1921 and 1998 Nottinghamshire hosted 47 first-class matches at the Town Ground in Worksop. The only hat-trick there by a Nottinghamshire bowler belonged to Harold Butler. The fast-medium right-armer took 952 wickets during his career, including Ewart Astill, George Dawkes and Haydon Smith in consecutive deliveries against Leicestershire. Butler recorded two further hat-tricks for Notts, both at Trent Bridge, against Surrey – also in 1937 – and against Hampshire in 1939, to join Alfred Shaw as the only players to take three for the county.

FRIDAY 12th JUNE 1964

Born in Dunbartonshire, Scotland, Peter Mark Such made his Nottinghamshire debut in 1982 against Middlesex at Lord's. The right-arm off-spinner went on to play 52 first-class games for the county, taking 138 wickets at 29.21. Such's best analysis was 6-123, against Kent at Trent Bridge in 1983. He moved to Leicestershire in 1987 and Essex three years later, where he gained international recognition with 11 Test match appearances for England.

THURSDAY 12th JUNE 1997

Nathan Astle's first innings at Trent Bridge, after joining Nottinghamshire for the summer, was against the touring Australians. Despite having already played 11 Tests at that time, the New Zealander had not faced his country's closest rivals before and went so close to a celebratory start before being dismissed by Glenn McGrath for 99. Rain ruined much of the drawn contest, which also featured hundreds by Matthew Elliott and Steve Waugh for the visitors.

THURSDAY 13th JUNE 1929

George Gunn enjoyed far from traditional 50th birthday celebrations. Batting for Nottinghamshire, against Worcestershire at New Road, he scored 164 not out. Born at Hucknall Torkard, he carried on playing for his county for another three years, by which time he'd scored a club-record 31,529 runs from 583 matches, at an average of 35.69.

FRIDAY 13th JUNE 2003

Nottinghamshire's first match in the newly-formed domestic Twenty20 competition ended in a six-wicket loss to Durham at Chester-le-Street. Skipper Jason Gallian made 62 in Notts' total of 157-7, which the home side chased down with five balls to spare.

TUESDAY 14th JUNE 1938

Don Bradman, generally acclaimed as being one of the greatest Test batsmen of all time, made six appearances at Trent Bridge. In his 11 innings for Australia in Nottingham, he scored an aggregate of 812 runs at an average of 81.20. Of his four centuries, the highest came in the 1938 Test, when he scored an undefeated 144 in the second innings of a draw.

FRIDAY 14th JUNE 1968

Beware the limping cricketer! Although in a losing cause, a half-fit Garfield Sobers scored his first Nottinghamshire century against Middlesex at Lord's. Hobbling throughout, having only been able to bowl 8.3 overs in the match, the captain scored exactly 100 in his side's ten-wicket defeat. Mike Harris, later to move to Nottinghamshire, scored 109 for the home side to set up the victory.

SUNDAY 14th JUNE 1987

Nottinghamshire defeated Glamorgan in a Refuge Assurance League match at Ebbw Vale but there was something for the home fans to cheer about as Geoff Holmes took a hat-trick by dismissing Paul Johnson, David Fraser-Darling and Bruce French.

FRIDAY 15th JUNE 1951

All-rounder Peter Harvey scored 3,632 runs for Nottinghamshire in 173 matches between 1947 and 1958. They came at an average of 18.53 and featured two centuries and nine half-centuries, with a best of 150 against Leicestershire at Grace Road in a drawn championship fixture.

MONDAY 15th JUNE 1959

Keith Miller was one of Australia's finest all-rounders, scoring almost 3,000 runs and taking 170 wickets in 55 Tests. After winding down his career – and in his 40th year – he accepted an invitation to play a one-off game for Nottinghamshire at home to Cambridge University. Miller scored 62 in the first innings but, second time around, in front of 5,000 spectators he scored a blistering century, ending on 102 not out. The match also saw Carlton Forbes make his debut for the county, picking up two wickets including Henry Blofeld, later a well-respected broadcaster and cricket commentator.

MONDAY 16th JUNE 2003

Nottinghamshire's first domestic Twenty20 home fixture ended in a seven-wicket victory over Lancashire. The visitors were bowled out in the final over for just 120, with Richard Logan taking 5-26. It would be eight years before those figures were bettered by another Notts bowler, Darren Pattinson. This inaugural success for the county was under the captaincy of Paul Franks.

TUESDAY 17th JUNE 1930

Sydney Copley didn't have much of a first-class career for Nottinghamshire. Playing just once, against Oxford University, he scored four and three then failed to take a wicket. However, his big moment came when he was used as a fielding substitute for England in the Trent Bridge Test against Australia. At mid-on, he pulled off a brilliant diving catch to dismiss the dangerous Stan McCabe and alter the complexion of the match. Copley's brilliance averted a possible defeat as England then went on to win.

SATURDAY 18th JUNE 1955

Born in Aspley, John Dennis Birch played 250 first-class matches for Nottinghamshire, scoring 8,673 runs at an average of 27.53. He also took 50 wickets with his medium-pace bowling, as well as playing 235 List A games, where he scored 3,793 runs and took 35 wickets. Birch played in the Notts side that won the 1987 NatWest Trophy, as well as the losing 1982 Benson and Hedges Cup final team.

TUESDAY 18th JUNE 1985

There was a well-deserved man of the match award for Nottinghamshire's Tim Robinson at the end of the first Ashes Test of the summer, against Australia at Headingley. The opener scored 175 in England's first innings, the highest of his four Test centuries.

SUNDAY 19th JUNE 1870

The only Nottinghamshire cricketer to be killed whilst playing for the county was George Summers. Born in Nottingham on 21 June 1844, he was an excellent fielder and more than capable defensive batsman. Summers was in his 18th first-class match when he was struck whilst batting on the third day of a game (15th June 1870) against MCC at Lord's. His first delivery, bowled by John Platts, struck him on the left side of his head. Summers dropped to the ground and – understandably – retired hurt. He left London to return home the following day but on the Sunday morning he died at his parents' house, 35 Station Street, Nottingham, two days before turning 26.

SUNDAY 19th JUNE 1977

The lowest score made against Nottinghamshire in List A cricket came at the County Ground, Northampton. Notts had struggled to make their way to 130-8 in their 40 overs but it was more than enough as the home side folded for just 43. Five different bowlers shared the wickets with Dilip Doshi's figures making the most interesting reading: 8-7-1-1.

TUESDAY 19th JUNE 2001

A little early in the year for fireworks! During a one-day international at Trent Bridge, noisy and excitable Pakistan spectators threw a firework on to the outfield prompting Australia's captain, Steve Waugh, to lead his side off. After a stoppage of 18 minutes, with order restored, play resumed and Pakistan eventually won by 36 runs.

MONDAY 20th JUNE 1983

Richard Hadlee usually came out on top whenever he played at Trent Bridge but he finished on the losing side against Pakistan in a World Cup match there. Although Hadlee had picked up the wicket of the dangerous Javed Miandad, another top-order batsman, Zaheer Abbas, scored an unbeaten 103 in Pakistan's 11-run victory over New Zealand.

SUNDAY 21st JUNE 1903

A dreadful day for the county side, as Yorkshire dismissed them for just 13 at Trent Bridge. Wilfred Rhodes (6-4) and Schofield Haigh (4-8) did the damage with the home side bowled out in just 15.5 overs. During the early stages of the match, with the visitors batting, Arthur Shrewsbury split his hand fielding at point. Yorkshire captain Lord Hawke allowed Isaac Harrison to officially replace the injured man. Harrison's contribution to the contest could hardly be described as significant – he was out for 0 in each innings!

SUNDAY 21st JUNE 1987

The first List A hat-trick taken by a Nottinghamshire bowler was secured by Kevin Saxelby. Playing against Worcestershire at Trent Bridge in the Refuge Assurance League 40-over competition, the fast-medium bowler sent back Steve Rhodes, Phil Neale and Neal Radford in successive deliveries.

THURSDAY 22nd JUNE 1893

On the opening day of Nottinghamshire's match against Gloucestershire, Charles Wright became the first player to be given out handled the ball, whilst representing the county. The ball had become lodged in his pads and he picked it out and handed it to a fielder, only to be sent on his way after the umpire upheld an appeal.

WEDNESDAY 22nd JUNE 1988

Derek Randall scored six one-day centuries for Nottinghamshire, topped by an undefeated 149 against Devon at Torquay. Helping his side through to the second round of the NatWest Trophy, Randall shared an unbroken fourth-wicket stand of 205 with John Birch – the county's largest in List A away from Trent Bridge.

WEDNESDAY 22nd JUNE 1994

Nottinghamshire's largest margin of victory in one-day action came at Jesmond when they defeated Northumberland by 228 runs in the NatWest Trophy. Paul Johnson scored 146 out of a total of 344-6 (60 overs) and then Kevin Evans swept through the home side (116 all out) to finish with figures of 7-3-10-6, the best by any Notts bowler in List A cricket.

SATURDAY 23rd JUNE 1979

The second ICC World Cup final was played at Lord's between England and West Indies, the defending champions. Nottinghamshire were represented by Derek Randall, who produced the first outstanding moment of the match, swooping brilliantly to run out the dangerous Gordon Greenidge. Sadly for Randall, who made 15 before being bowled by Colin Croft later in the day, England were emphatically defeated by 92 runs.

MONDAY 24th JUNE 1946

England's first post-war Test (and first for seven years) was a personal triumph for Joe Hardstaff junior. The Nottinghamshire batsman became the first to score a double century against India at Lord's, reaching 205 not out in a ten-wicket victory. It was the fourth and final time Hardstaff passed three figures for his country and first since making 169 not out against Australia in 1938.

FRIDAY 24th JUNE 1977

Nottinghamshire lifted some mid-season silverware when they secured the four-team Tilcon Trophy at Harrogate. After defeating Middlesex in the semi-final of the 55-overs tournament, Mike Smedley's side beat Derbyshire by 26 runs in the final. Nirmal Nanan's 60 was the top score of the game with Clive Rice taking 3-49 to thwart Derbyshire, who had eliminated Yorkshire the day before.

TUESDAY 24th JUNE 1986

Stuart Christopher John Broad emulated his father, Chris Broad, by beginning his first-class career elsewhere and then moving to Trent Bridge. Born in Nottingham, he began with Leicestershire but switched counties at the end of the 2007 campaign. The right-arm fast bowler and left-handed batsman firmly established himself in the England sides at Test, ODI and Twenty20 level, restricting his availability for Nottinghamshire, but he played a pivotal role in the county's 2010 championship win by turning in match-winning bowling performances against Somerset and Warwickshire.

SATURDAY 25th JUNE 1921

Two long-standing records resulted from the match against the touring Australians at Trent Bridge. Right-handed New South Wales batsman Charles Macartney made the highest individual score ever compiled at Trent Bridge. His 345 came in 232 minutes, with 47 fours and four sixes. After conceding 675, Nottinghamshire twice fell cheaply, for 58 and for 100, meaning the margin of defeat was an innings and 517 runs, their heaviest of all time.

MONDAY 25th JUNE 1928

Nottinghamshire set a new record for a side scoring the most runs with only three wickets lost. At The Butts Ground in Coventry they declared on 656-3 against Warwickshire, with four batsmen scoring hundreds. With an opening stand worth 245, George Gunn made 148 and "Dodger" Whysall, 132. Skipper Arthur Carr missed out somewhat, by only reaching 58 but Willis Walker, with 146 not out and Fred Barratt's career-best 139 not out made it a tough experience for the home attack. Warwickshire responded with a couple of centuries of their own and were indebted to a final day lost to rain as they escaped with a draw.

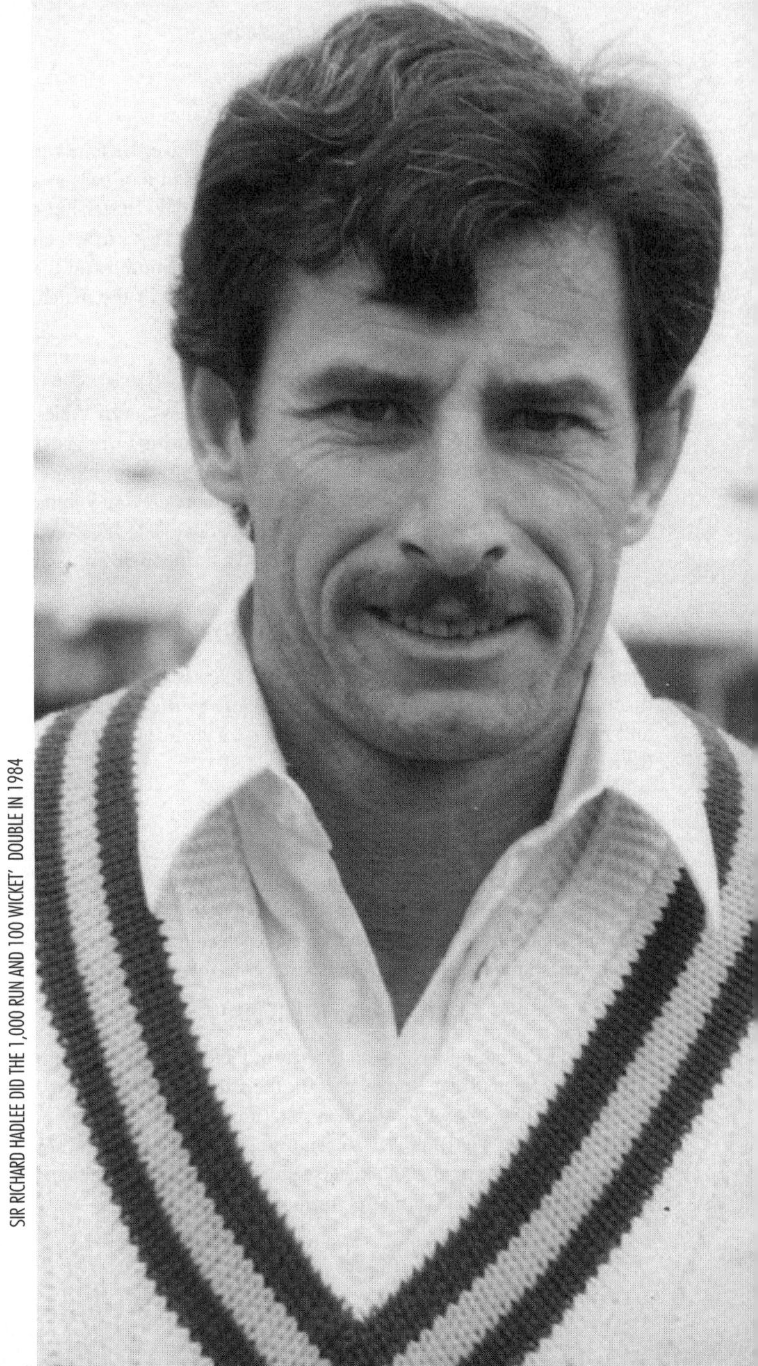

SIR RICHARD HADLEE DID THE 1,000 RUN AND 100 WICKET' DOUBLE IN 1984

MONDAY 25th JUNE 1956

Emulating the 1893 feat of FJ Shacklock, Alan Walker became the second Nottinghamshire bowler to take four wickets in four balls in a first-class fixture. Walker's achievement spanned both of Leicestershire's innings at Grace Road. He ended the first by bowling Jack Firth, then removed Gerry Lester, Maurice Tompkin and Gerald Smithson at the start of the second. The Australian bowler took eight in the match, which Notts won by nine wickets.

FRIDAY 25th JUNE 1971

Jason Edward Riche Gallian was born in Manly, New South Wales, and captained Australia's Young Cricketers before moving to England to study and play for Oxford University then Lancashire. Having qualified for England, he made three Test appearances before joining Notts in 1997. In 144 matches for the Trent Bridge side he scored 8,445 runs at an average of 38.73 and he scored a further 3,585 runs in List A competition.

SATURDAY 26th JUNE 1926

Harold Larwood's Test debut came at Lord's against Australia. He dismissed Charles Macartney and Jack Gregory in the first innings and Herbie Collins in the second but didn't get a chance to bat in the drawn contest.

SATURDAY 26th JUNE 1976

Two players who would enjoy long and successful careers on the Trent Bridge staff made their debuts in a first-class friendly against Cambridge University. Seam bowler Kevin Cooper took four wickets in each of the students' innings, whilst Bruce French enjoyed a competent match behind the stumps, taking three catches in the routine victory.

FRIDAY 27th JUNE 1980

Kevin Peter Pietersen was born on this day in Pietermaritzburg, South Africa. Brought to Trent Bridge in 2001, the tall right-hander played 58 first-class matches for Nottinghamshire, scoring 4,719 runs, at an average of 55.51. He compiled 16 centuries, with a best of 254 not out against Middlesex in 2002. Pietersen scored four List A hundreds before leaving at the end of the 2004 season.

SATURDAY 27th JUNE 1992

Two Nottinghamshire players turned in career-best performances during a three-day match against Cambridge University at Trent Bridge. Opener Wayne Dessaur scored 148, the largest of his three centuries for Notts, whilst slow left-arm spinner James Hindson, on debut, claimed 5-42 in a match won by 162 runs.

TUESDAY 27th JUNE 1995

Man of the match in Nottinghamshire's NatWest Trophy success over Scotland at Trent Bridge was Andy Pick. The paceman recorded a hat-trick, all three lbw, to claim 5-23.

TUESDAY 28th JUNE 1960

Chasing 215 to win, Nottinghamshire came up just short in a championship match against Sussex at Trent Bridge. At 183-9 the home side looked well beaten but a tense, nail-biting stand of 30 between John Springall and Thomas Atkinson took them to the brink of victory before Atkinson was out lbw, leaving the south coast county to celebrate a one-run victory.

THURSDAY 28th JUNE 1984

After five years in the Gloucestershire first team, Chris Broad was given a Test debut in his first season as a Nottinghamshire player. The left-handed opening batsman began his international career by making 55 against the West Indies at Lord's, before being dismissed by Malcolm Marshall.

MONDAY 28th JUNE 1993

A century from Paul Johnson not only helped Nottinghamshire to an eight-wicket win over Glamorgan at Swansea – it also earned him a share of the Walter Lawrence Trophy as joint-fastest of the season. Johnson's ton came from just 73 balls, a mark matched by a batsman playing in the same match, Glamorgan's Matthew Maynard.

THURSDAY 29th JUNE 1950

No-one has scored more double centuries for Nottinghamshire than Reg Simpson. The prolific batsman reached that landmark on nine separate occasions, although he repeatedly failed to reach 250. His highest score came at Trent Bridge, against Worcestershire, when he made 243 not out.

SUNDAY 29th JUNE 1980

Peter Hacker took 51 wickets for Nottinghamshire in List A cricket. The left-arm fast-medium bowler produced his best figures in a John Player League match against Essex at Chelmsford. Hacker's figures of 7.3-1-16-6 helped his side to an 18-run victory.

MONDAY 29th JUNE 1987

Richard Hadlee's only hat-trick for Nottinghamshire came at the St Lawrence Ground in Canterbury. Following on, Kent sped to defeat when Taylor, Aslett and Tavare were removed at the top of the order to leave the score 9-3.

WEDNESDAY 30th JUNE 1886

In a match that was enjoyed by both captains, Nottinghamshire secured a draw against Gloucestershire at Moreton-in-Marsh. For Gloucestershire, WG Grace took seven wickets and scored an unbeaten 92 but with his side up against it, Arthur Shrewsbury Sr carried his bat in the visitors' second innings, scoring 227 not out in seven hours and 45 minutes.

SATURDAY 30th JUNE 1984

Nottinghamshire fielded four debutants against Cambridge University at Trent Bridge. David Fraser-Darling took three wickets in the match and Kevin Evans bagged two. Batsman Mick Newell scored 76 on his first appearance for the county but there was less to celebrate for Steven Mee. Although the 19-year-old took match figures of 2-63, he failed to score a run and didn't play another first-class match in his career. In the students' second innings, Rob Andrew, later to play for England and the British Lions at rugby union, scored an unbeaten 101.

SATURDAY 30th JUNE 2000

On the opening day of Trent Bridge's Weekend of Legends, a Sir Richard Hadlee XI defeated a Sir Garfield Sobers XI by seven wickets. Nottinghamshire's two former cricketing knights had each put together a side featuring some of the very best players in the world. The following day, in another star-studded spectacular, the England Masters defeated the Australian Masters, with former Nottinghamshire players Derek Randall, Bruce French, Tim Robinson and Chris Lewis in the winning XI.

NOTTINGHAMSHIRE CCC
On This Day

JULY

WEDNESDAY 1st JULY 1970

The highest of Mike Smedley's 28 centuries for Nottinghamshire came at Cardiff, when he made 149 against Glamorgan. His unbeaten five in the second innings, although not nearly as significant, was enough to earn an eight-wicket victory.

THURSDAY 1st JULY 1999

Chris Read made his Test debut for England against New Zealand at Edgbaston becoming England's youngest wicketkeeper of the century at just 20 years 325 days. Read's first dismissal was a catch off the bowling of Mark Butcher to dismiss Nathan Astle, a former Nottinghamshire team-mate. England eventually won by seven wickets with Read getting a total of eight victims in the match, including six (five caught, one stumped) in the second innings, a record for a debutant.

FRIDAY 1st JULY 2011

Tamim Iqbal became the first Bangladesh international to play for Nottinghamshire when he made five appearances in the Twenty20 competition. The aggressive, left-handed opener scored 104 runs at an average of just over 20 but he fell for just eight on his debut, away against Derbyshire.

FRIDAY 2nd JULY 1954

Repeating his feat of three years earlier, Reg Simpson scored a Test century on his county ground. The Nottinghamshire opener made a first innings 101 – his fourth and final Test hundred – as England piled on 558-6 declared on their way to victory by an innings. Denis Compton also made 278, the highest Test score ever achieved in Nottingham.

SUNDAY 2nd JULY 1995

Paul Pollard's highest career one-day score, 132 not out, helped seal a six-wicket win over Somerset in an AXA Equity and Law League clash at Trent Bridge. Making their Notts debuts were Usman Afzaal, who didn't bat but took 1-38, and medium-fast bowler Jamie Hart, who took 1-48. In an unusual quirk of fate, Hart opened the bowling with Bobby Chapman, meaning that both strike bowlers were the sons of former Nottingham Forest footballers: Paul Hart and Sammy Chapman.

MONDAY 2nd JULY 2001

Despite 20 wickets falling on the first day, Nottinghamshire's match against Worcestershire at New Road culminated in them making a match-winning 461-3 on the final day, their highest fourth-innings total to win a championship match. The contest had been set up by first-innings hundreds from Graeme Hick for Worcestershire and Kevin Pietersen for the visitors. Phil Weston's 192 looked to give Worcestershire the advantage before Greg Blewett (134 not out), Darren Bicknell (104), John Morris (94), Usman Afzaal (88) and Paul Johnson (26 not out) turned the tables with an astonishing and record-breaking counter-attack.

THURSDAY 3rd JULY 1884

Despite playing 15 Tests for England as a specialist batsman, left-hander William Scotton only scored four centuries in his career. The highest of them, 134, came whilst representing an England XI against the touring Australians at Huddersfield. Two of his other hundreds came for Nottinghamshire, with the other made for MCC at Lord's.

TUESDAY 3rd JULY 1951

Richard John Hadlee was born in St Albans, Christchurch, New Zealand, and was an established Test player when he joined Nottinghamshire in 1978. As a right-arm swing bowler, there have been few that possessed his match-winning capabilities, as his 431 Test wickets from 86 appearances would testify. He was also a good enough left-handed batsman to score 14 first-class hundreds and be classed as a true all-rounder. For Nottinghamshire, Hadlee played in two championship-winning sides, as well as playing a starring role in their 1987 NatWest Trophy win at Lord's. Of all his statistics for the county, his bowling average is the most phenomenal – 622 first-class wickets at just 14.51, 231 List A wickets at 17.99. He was knighted in 1990 for his services to cricket and in 2009 was inducted into the ICC Hall of Fame.

SATURDAY 3rd JULY 1982

Notts progressed in the NatWest Trophy when they defeated Sussex by nine wickets at Hove. The victory was set up by skipper Clive Rice, who took the man of the match award for his figures of 6-18, the best of his one-day career.

SATURDAY 4th JULY 1981

Whilst all around him failed, Clive Rice scored a brilliant century against Hampshire at Bournemouth. The Nottinghamshire captain made an undefeated 105 from an all-out total of 143. Tim Robinson, with ten, was the only other batsman to make double figures. Notts fared even worse in their second innings, dismissed for just 99. In mitigation, they were blown away by West Indian Malcolm Marshall and former Derbyshire man Keith Stevenson, who each took nine wickets in the match. Gaining experience of English conditions, one of the umpires was Shakoor Rana, the Pakistan official who became embroiled in a finger-wagging row with Mike Gatting, the England captain, six years later.

WEDNESDAY 4th JULY 2001

Bilal Shafayat was denied a century on his Nottinghamshire debut when he was trapped lbw by former England spinner Phil Tufnell. Against Middlesex at Trent Bridge, the youngster was still six days away from his 17th birthday when he fell for 72.

FRIDAY 4th JULY 2008

Nottinghamshire batsman David Hussey made his ODI debut for Australia against the West Indies in Basseterre, St Kitts. Batting in a side that also included his elder brother Michael Hussey, the right-hander scored 50 from just 51 deliveries, as his side sneaked a victory by just one run.

SUNDAY 5th JULY 1970

Nottinghamshire played four John Player League matches at the (appropriately-named) John Player Ground, on Aspley Lane, Nottingham. They won two and lost two, with the only century being scored in the first match by Mike Harris. The Notts opener made 104 not out, as his side reached 209-3, enough to defeat Hampshire by 34 runs.

THURSDAY 5th JULY 2001

Twenty-four-year-old Usman Afzaal made three Test appearances for England in 2001. The left-handed Nottinghamshire batsman scored four and two on debut, against Australia at Edgbaston. He made 54 later in the same series, at The Oval, and also took the wicket of Adam Gilchrist with his slow left-arm spin, but wasn't selected again.

WEDNESDAY 6th JULY 2011

England defeated Sri Lanka in an ODI at Trent Bridge by ten wickets. Chasing a revised Duckworth-Lewis total of 171, openers Alastair Cook (95) and Craig Kieswetter (72 not out), saw England to victory. Earlier, Nottinghamshire's Stuart Broad had taken 2-37 in the Sri Lankan innings.

SATURDAY 7th JULY 1928

It was a regal affair at Trent Bridge as His Majesty King George V visited during Nottinghamshire's match against the West Indies. Asked what the King had said to him, fast bowler Harold Larwood replied: "He said, how old are you son?" The 23-year-old Larwood took three wickets in the drawn contest.

WEDNESDAY 7th JULY 2004

The highest score made by a Nottinghamshire batsman in the first nine years of the domestic Twenty20 competition was by Mark Ealham. Against Yorkshire, at Trent Bridge, he smashed five fours and nine sixes in a 35-ball 91 that propelled his side to victory.

TUESDAY 8th JULY 1952

After making his Test debut in India the previous winter, Cyril Poole enjoyed being reunited with the cricketers of that country. When the tourists came to Trent Bridge to face Nottinghamshire, Poole made the highest score of his career, 222 not out. During that 1952 season the left-handed Poole scored 1,700 runs at 38.63, with three centuries and nine 50s, yet was unable to reclaim his place in the Test side.

SUNDAY 8th JULY 2007

Although a positive outcome looked unlikely from the start, Nottinghamshire's match against Essex at Chelmsford did make its way into the record books. Having seen their opponents pile up a first-innings total of 700-9 declared over the first two days, the visitors then found the surface equally productive. A career-best 240 from Chris Read, following on from Samit Patel's 117, Mark Wagh's 107, and backed up by 97 from Graeme Swann, sent the statisticians into overdrive as Nottinghamshire made 791 all out – their highest first-class total.

SUNDAY 9th JULY 1893

Aged just 37, William Scotton took his own life at his residence in St John's Wood, London. Said to have been in a low, depressed condition since losing his place in the Nottinghamshire side, he had been working on the groundstaff of MCC at the time of his death. He had made 152 appearances for Notts, scoring over 4,000 runs with two centuries and had played 15 Tests for England between 1881 and 1887.

THURSDAY 10th JULY 1879

The lowest score made against Notts is 16 – by Surrey in 1880 and, a year earlier, by Derbyshire at Trent Bridge. Responding to the home side's 159, Derbyshire were undone by two bowlers, Fred Morley and Alf Shaw. In an innings including six ducks Morley recorded figures of 7-7, with his partner returning 3-9. Following on, the visitors only made 44, with the same two bowlers each collecting a further five wickets.

SUNDAY 11th JULY 2010

There was nothing to choose between the two sides when Nottinghamshire Outlaws met Northamptonshire Steelbacks in their two Twenty20 meetings. Having tied their clash at Trent Bridge three weeks earlier, they met again at the County Ground, Northampton. Chasing the Outlaws' total of 144-7, the home side needed ten from the final over for the win – but could only score nine. Lightning did strike twice, as the game ended in yet another tie.

MONDAY 12th JULY 1915

Born in Selston, Arthur Jepson was a true all-round sportsman who played football for a number of clubs either side of the Second World War as a goalkeeper. Mansfield Town, Port Vale, Stoke City and Lincoln City were all grateful recipients of his athleticism, as were Nottinghamshire County Cricket Club, with whom he played 390 first-class matches, taking 1,050 wickets with his right-arm fast-medium bowling. His best performance was 8-45 against Leicestershire and he registered one century, 130 against Worcestershire. After retiring as a player he turned to umpiring and stood in four Tests, the first of which was the England against the West Indies match at Trent Bridge in 1966.

TUESDAY 12th JULY 1932

The best-ever bowling performance against Nottinghamshire was recorded by Yorkshire's Hedley Verity at Headingley. Batting again, after taking a first-innings lead of 71, Notts reached 44-0 before the introduction of the slow left-arm spinner. He then recorded the astonishing figures of 19.4-16-10-10 – which included a hat-trick of Willis Walker, Charles Harris and George Gunn – as the visitors capsized to 67 all out and an eventual defeat.

SATURDAY 13th JULY 1935

Nottinghamshire's Joe Hardstaff junior followed his father into the England Test side with a debut against South Africa at Leeds. Scores of 10 and 0 meant that it would be another year before he would be involved again but he did go on to play for his country on 23 occasions.

SATURDAY 13th JULY 1957

On the opening day of Nottinghamshire's match with Derbyshire at Trent Bridge, John Clay became the only outfield player from the county, in the 20th century, to take six catches in an innings. Five of Clay's victims fell to the bowling of Gamini Goonesena (7-76) with the other coming from fellow spinner Bruce Dooland.

SATURDAY 13th JULY 1974

Succumbing to an innings defeat by Yorkshire at Worksop, Nottinghamshire showed their vulnerability against both seam and spin. In their first innings score of just 94, they were blown away by five-wicket hauls from Dennis Schofield and Arthur Robinson – the latter collecting the wickets of Mike Smedley, Jack Bond and Philip Wilkinson in a hat-trick. Second time around the home county could only make 87 with Geoff Cope and Don Wilson each taking five-fors.

FRIDAY 14th JULY 1978

Nottinghamshire slipped to a 152-run defeat to Worcestershire, bringing a disappointing end to their 13-year association with the Elm Avenue Ground in Newark. Between 1966 and 1978 the county had played a total of 15 first-team matches there, winning all four one-day contests but unable to win any of their 11 first-class fixtures.

FRIDAY 15th JULY 1977

Born in Morley, Western Australia, David John Hussey joined Nottinghamshire for the start of the 2004 season. Scoring 1,315 runs at an average of 69.21, with seven centuries that summer, was ample confirmation of his talent and ensured he would be utilised as the county's overseas player whenever available for the rest of the decade. A stylish and sometimes devastating right-handed batsman and off-break bowler, he had to wait until 2008 before making his Twenty20 and ODI debuts for Australia. As well as hitting three of his first four career double-hundreds as a Notts player, he also helped the side to two county championships and captained them to the 2010 Twenty20 Finals Day.

SATURDAY 15th JULY 1989

A tense conclusion to the Benson and Hedges Cup final at Lord's saw Nottinghamshire sneak past Essex from the last delivery after Alan Lilley's 95 not out had lifted his side to 243-7 from their 55 overs. Notts lost openers Broad and Pollard early in their reply but experienced trio Robinson (86), Johnson (54) and Randall (49) all kept the chase alive. Eight were needed from the last over and four from the final ball. Forty-year-old Eddie Hemmings stepped back to cut John Lever away to the backward-point boundary to give Notts their only title in the competition.

WEDNESDAY 16th JULY 1997

The first Nottinghamshire hat-trick for ten years was taken by Paul Franks at Trent Bridge against Warwickshire. Trevor Penney was his first victim, caught behind, then Dougie Brown and Graeme Welch were both bowled in the first innings of a drawn championship fixture.

MONDAY 17th JULY 1893

In just his 21st match Nottinghamshire's Arthur Shrewsbury became the first batsman to reach an aggregate of 1,000 runs in Test cricket. He went in to the first Test against Australia at Lord's with 993 runs under his belt but he celebrated in style by making 106 in the first innings of the drawn match. Shrewsbury only played twice more, concluding his Test career with 1,277 runs at an average of 35.47.

MONDAY 17th JULY 1939

Resuming unbeaten on 263, made on the Saturday, Walter Keeton went on to reach 312 not out, in Nottinghamshire's eventual 560-9 declared against Middlesex. His innings, the highest-ever score made by a batsman for the county, was achieved at The Oval as Middlesex's usual home venue, Lord's, was being used for the annual fixture between Eton and Harrow. Notts won by an innings, Bill Voce taking 7-70 and 3-69 to complete a ten-wicket haul in the match.

THURSDAY 17th JULY 1975

Nottinghamshire's player of the year in 2010 and 2011, Andre Ryan Adams, was born in Auckland, New Zealand. With devastating control, he established himself as one of the leading swing bowlers of his generation as his 68 wickets – including the final all-important two – led Notts to their 2010 county title. His only Test appearance, against England in 2002, had been accompanied by 42 ODI outings for the Black Caps but his decision to commit to county cricket became a personal success story. A thunderous hitter of a cricket ball, he hit more sixes than any other player on the county circuit during 2011.

MONDAY 18th JULY 1994

Although Notts still lost to Somerset by more than 100 runs at Taunton, they at least went down fighting, and created a little bit of history in the process. Delaying the inevitable, Jimmy Adams and Kevin Evans put on a new county record stand of 170 for the ninth wicket, with the West Indian making 144 not out, his highest score for the county, with Evans adding 77.

FRIDAY 18th JULY 2008

As the most in-form new-ball bowler in the country, Nottinghamshire's Darren Pattinson was given a Test debut for England against South Africa at Headingley. Having played only 11 first-class matches – five in Australia for Victoria and six for Notts – he took 2-95, as the tourists ran up a score of 522 all out. Sadly the faith that had been shown in his selection quickly dissipated as he was omitted from the next match.

WEDNESDAY 19th JULY 1876

John Richmond Gunn emulated the feat of his uncle, Billy, by playing Test cricket for England. Younger brother George would later become the third Gunn to achieve international status. Born in Hucknall Torkard, he was a left-handed batsman and a left-arm bowler, capable of bowling slow spin, or medium-paced deliveries. For Nottinghamshire, JR made 489 appearances and scored 23,194 runs at an average of 34.36. He registered 40 centuries, top-scoring with a knock of 294 against Leicestershire in 1903.

SATURDAY 19th JULY 2003

Trent Bridge was all dressed up for a party with everyone there except the host! The first Twenty20 Finals Day was held in Nottingham but the Outlaws failed to advance beyond the group stage. Surrey Lions beat Warwickshire Bears in the final, with Gloucestershire Gladiators and Leicestershire Foxes knocked out in the semis and left to enjoy the evening entertainment, which was provided by Atomic Kitten.

SUNDAY 19th JULY 2009

David Hussey's only one-day century for Nottinghamshire, in his first eight years with the county, eventually counted for nothing. In scoring 120 not out and putting on 204 with Matt Wood (91) the Australian helped his side reach 247-5 from just 26 overs. The wet conditions, which had already interrupted the Trent Bridge fixture against Somerset, returned early in the visitors' reply. Hussey's assault had included six fours and ten sixes and lasted for just 61 balls.

TUESDAY 20th JULY 1886

The largest of Arthur Shrewsbury's three Test centuries came at Lord's, 164 for England against Australia. He was last out, as his side reached 353, enough to win the match by an innings.

FRIDAY 20th JULY 1934

Walter Keeton's two Test appearances were separated by five years. The Nottinghamshire opening bat scored 25 and 12 on debut against Australia at Leeds and then had to wait until 1939 before playing against the West Indies at The Oval, where he made 0 and 20.

CLIVE RICE CAPTAINED NOTTS TO TWO COUNTY CHAMPIONSHIP TITLES

THURSDAY 20th JULY 1950

Trent Bridge cricket-watchers were treated to a batting master-class as the third Test between England and West Indies began in Nottingham. Frank Worrell scored 261 and Everton Weekes made 129 for the tourists but home fans were then both delighted and dismayed as Nottinghamshire's Reg Simpson batted superbly, only to be run out six runs short of a century on his own ground. The West Indies went on to win by a comprehensive ten wickets.

THURSDAY 20th JULY 2000

Nottinghamshire's Paul Franks made one ODI appearance for England but it did take place at his own county headquarters. A full Trent Bridge crowd saw him open the bowling against the West Indies but despite returning tidy figures he was unable to pick up a wicket and was dismissed for four as the tourists won a last-ball thriller by just three runs.

SATURDAY 21st JULY 1951

Fred Trueman was a fearsome sight for opposition batsmen. On the opening morning of a championship game against Nottinghamshire at Trent Bridge he reduced the home side to 18-6, aided by a hat-trick of Reg Simpson, Alan Armitage and Peter Harvey. The Yorkshire quickie returned figures of 8-53 as the tail wagged to reach 122. An unbeaten 194 from Len Hutton set up the White Rose county for a nine-wicket win.

WEDNESDAY 21st JULY 1982

Eddie Hemmings played 518 first-class matches and scored just one century, which came for Nottinghamshire against Yorkshire at the Town Ground, Worksop. He arrived at the crease with Notts on 127-7 and reached an undefeated 127 as the innings closed on 329-9 declared. Hemmings took five wickets in the match also but was unable to prevent his side slipping to defeat.

WEDNESDAY 21st JULY 1999

On the opening day of a PPP Healthcare County Championship match against Kent at Trent Bridge, Nottinghamshire's Wayne Noon broke a county record. The wicketkeeper became the first Notts glove-man to take seven catches in an innings.

WEDNESDAY 21st JULY 2004

A dramatic finish to a totesport League 40-over match at Hove saw Nottinghamshire grab a share of the points thanks to the bowling of Ryan Sidebottom. Batting first, Notts scored 260-4, with Russell Warren making 78 and Jason Gallian 77. Sussex's reply went right down to the final delivery, which arrived with the scores level and last man James Kirtley on strike. Sidebottom's delivery clattered into the stumps to earn his side an unexpected tie.

WEDNESDAY 22nd JULY 1987

The County Ground, Derby, was the venue for the highest score of Mick Newell's first-class career. The right-handed batsman, opening the innings, made an undefeated 203 for Nottinghamshire against Derbyshire, setting his side up for victory by an innings and 33 runs. In 1987 Newell topped a thousand runs for the only time, hitting 1,034 at an average of 39.03 with three centuries.

WEDNESDAY 22nd JULY 1998

On the eve of the fourth Test of the series between England and South Africa, former Nottinghamshire all-rounder Sir Garfield Sobers formally opened the new Radcliffe Road Stand and Trent Bridge Cricket Centre. Built by Sol Construction and designed by Maber Associates, the new facility had been put together at a cost of £7.2million.

THURSDAY 22nd JULY 1999

With a cunningly disguised slower ball, learned from former Notts colleague Franklyn Stephenson, New Zealand's Chris Cairns got one over on his current county team-mate Chris Read in a Test at Lord's. The viciously dipping delivery saw the England keeper turn away from what seemed a head-high full toss, only for it to crash into the base of the stumps.

THURSDAY 22nd JULY 2010

Stuart Broad took the first eight-wicket haul of his career when helping Nottinghamshire to a ten-wicket victory over Warwickshire at Edgbaston. The pace bowler, playing between his England commitments, finished with figures of 8-52 in the home side's second innings, having taken 3-79 in the first.

SATURDAY 23rd JULY 1949

It's probably fair to say that Johannesburg-born Clive Edward Butler Rice, over 13 years as a player – and later as coach – gave Nottinghamshire sensational value. In 283 first-class matches he scored 17,053 runs and took 476 wickets, with one-day appearances totalling 274 games, 8,666 runs and 291 wickets. As captain, he led the county to two county championships and the NatWest Trophy success of 1987.

FRIDAY 24th JULY 1863

The first Nottinghamshire player to score a century and take two six-wicket hauls in the same match was John Jackson. The right-arm fast bowler took 6-23 against Kent then, batting at eight, scored exactly 100 – the only century of his career. The home side were dismissed for just 58 in their first innings and could make no more than 45 second time around, with Jackson picking up 6-20. It would be 124 years before the same feat was equalled by Richard Hadlee, against Somerset at Trent Bridge.

FRIDAY 24th JULY 1931

A unique occurrence in first-class cricket took place at Edgbaston, where Warwickshire were entertaining Nottinghamshire. Aged 52, Notts batsman George Gunn scored 183 and his son, 26-year-old George Vernon Gunn, made 100 not out, his maiden century for the county. It is the only instance of father and son scoring hundreds in the same innings.

SATURDAY 24th JULY 1982

Nottinghamshire were defeated by Somerset in the Benson and Hedges Cup final at Lord's, their first-ever one-day final. Put in to bat, Notts were bowled out for a disappointing 130, with Clive Rice top scoring on 27 and only four other batsmen reaching double figures. The Cidermen raced to a nine-wicket success, Mike Hendrick getting the only wicket to fall.

MONDAY 25th JULY 1949

In just his second Test, Nottinghamshire's Reg Simpson scored his first international hundred. Batting at Old Trafford against New Zealand, he scored 103 in an innings that contained 11 fours and three sixes.

SIR GARFIELD SOBERS, SCORER OF SIX SIXES IN AN OVER IN 1968

THURSDAY 25th JULY 1963

Nottinghamshire's Brian Bolus made his Test debut against the West Indies at Headingley. Opening alongside Surrey's Mickey Stewart, he drove the first ball he received, from Wes Hall, to the straight on-side boundary. Bolus fell to the same bowler for 14 in the first innings and to Garfield Sobers for 43 in the second.

MONDAY 25th JULY 1966

After playing 108 first-class matches, including 83 for Nottinghamshire which brought 170 wickets, slow left-arm spinner Keith Gillhouley was removed from the attack in a Trent Bridge match against Gloucestershire. Umpire Oswald "Lofty" Herman, at square leg, raised doubts about the legality of some deliveries and after consultation with Notts captain Norman Hill, the bowler was taken off. Gillhouley, 31, didn't play another first-class match.

FRIDAY 25th JULY 1980

Playing his first match for two years, after stepping down to captain the second XI, 43-year-old Bob White spun Nottinghamshire to victory over Derbyshire at Worksop. The veteran followed up his first innings 4-33 with 6-24 as the local rivals were dismissed for just 54.

FRIDAY 25th JULY 1997

The 17th and final time that a Nottinghamshire bowler recorded a hat-trick in the 20th century was by Chris Tolley at Grace Road against Leicestershire. On the third day, the left-arm medium-pace bowler sent back Darren Maddy, Paul Nixon and James Ormond in successive deliveries. Tolley's achievement came just nine days after team-mate Paul Franks had taken three in three against Warwickshire.

MONDAY 26th JULY 1943

Amritt Harrichand "Harry" Latchman was born in Jamaica but moved to England as a young child and went to school in Shepherd's Bush, West London. A right-handed batsman and leg-spin bowler, he played for Middlesex for nine seasons before bringing his cheery smile and engaging personality to Trent Bridge in 1974. Over the next three years he played 40 first-class and nine one-day matches before joining Cambridgeshire, on his way to pursuing a coaching career.

SATURDAY 26th JULY 1947

Aged 34, Nottinghamshire's Harold Butler made his England Test debut against South Africa at Headingley. He took 4-34 in the first innings and 3-32 in the second in a ten-wicket victory.

SATURDAY 26th JULY 1986

"Can anybody keep wicket?" was the cry after Nottinghamshire's Bruce French was struck on the head by a delivery from his county colleague Richard Hadlee, in the England v New Zealand Test at Lord's. He had to retire hurt without scoring and still wasn't fit enough to take the gloves later. Team-mate Bill Athey kept wicket first but, with the agreement of Kiwi captain Jeremy Coney, 45-year-old former England wicketkeeper Bob Taylor took over. The next day, a more logical replacement, Hampshire's Bobby Parks, stood in until French was able to return. None of the four were involved in a single dismissal as the match was drawn.

MONDAY 26th JULY 2004

For the first time, a championship match at Trent Bridge saw both teams pass 600 in their first innings. Hampshire made 641-4 declared, thanks to an unbeaten 301 from John Crawley and a century from Australia's Michael Clarke. Nottinghamshire's response was equally emphatic with David Hussey (170), Mark Ealham (113 not out) and Darren Bicknell (103) scoring tons of their own in a total of 612. Needless to say, the match was drawn.

MONDAY 27th JULY 1840

The first official inter-county match at Trent Bridge was between Notts and Sussex. The visitors spoiled the party by winning by 14 runs after they scored 115 and 73, the home county making 85 and 89.

TUESDAY 27th JULY 1880

A good day for two of Nottinghamshire's bowlers – Fred Morley's 7-9 and 3-6 from Alf Shaw condemned Surrey to an all-out total of just 16 at The Oval. The home side made 185 in their second knock but still lost by an innings.

SUNDAY 27th JULY 1930

Affectionately known as "Bomber", Bryan Douglas Wells was born in Gloucester and found his way into first-class cricket with his home county in 1951. Nine years later he joined Nottinghamshire, where he made 151 appearances, scoring 1,281 runs at the lower end of the batting order but taking 429 wickets with his off-breaks. His best performance with the ball was 7-34, against Worcestershire in 1963.

TUESDAY 28th JULY 1936

Perhaps the most famous Nottinghamshire cricketer of all time was born in Bridgetown, Barbados. Garfield St Aubrun Sobers was already the holder of the highest individual Test score when he joined the county in 1968. By the end of his first season at Trent Bridge he'd made a further long-lasting entry into the record books by hitting six sixes in an over against Glamorgan. The West Indian all-rounder made 107 first-class appearances for Notts, scoring 7,041 runs at 48.89 and taking 281 wickets at 25.62.

TUESDAY 28th JULY 1970

Zimbabwean leg-spin and googly bowler Paul Andrew Strang was born in Bulawayo. He joined Nottinghamshire for the 1998 season, taking 30 wickets in 13 first-class matches. His best performance with the ball came in an AXA League match against Warwickshire at Edgbaston when he ran through the Bears' middle order to take 6-32.

THURSDAY 28th JULY 1977

In the year of her Silver Jubilee, Her Majesty Queen Elizabeth II visited Trent Bridge and was introduced to all of the players, including Nottinghamshire's Derek Randall, ahead of the third Ashes Test between England and Australia.

FRIDAY 29th JULY 1977

After an incident that left legendary commentator John Arlott saying "he's leaving the field with tears in his eyes", Derek Randall was run out for 13 for England against Australia at Trent Bridge. Desperate to do well in front of his own supporters, the Nottinghamshire batsman was stranded after a mix-up involving Geoff Boycott, who made partial amends by scoring a century of his own.

WEDNESDAY 29th JULY 1987

Nottinghamshire completed the significant business of the day by defeating Derbyshire in the quarter-final of the NatWest Trophy at Derby. Notts scored 268-8, losing their way in the last over of their innings, with Martin Jean-Jacques taking a hat-trick of wickets: Hadlee, Birch and French. The home side could only make 211 all out in reply. It was the third time in the same season (previously against Leicestershire and Glamorgan) that French had been involved in an opposition hat-trick.

SUNDAY 30th JULY 1989

Kevin Saxelby set a new record for English domestic one-day cricket when he became the first bowler to take five wickets in an innings in four consecutive Sunday League matches. The Nottinghamshire fast bowler took 5-36 against Essex, following on from 5-24 v Warwickshire, 6-30 v Leicestershire and 5-45 v Northamptonshire. All of the matches were won and, unsurprisingly, Saxelby's 29 wickets that season made him the country's leading wicket-taker in the competition.

MONDAY 30th JULY 2001

On the final day of a drawn contest against Derbyshire at the County Ground, Kevin Pietersen advanced his career-high score to 218 not out. Batting with him was John Morris, who scored his second hundred of the match, ending on an unbeaten 136, as the pair set a new record for the county's sixth wicket of 372.

SATURDAY 30th JULY 2011

How fitting that the first-ever Test match hat-trick to be recorded at Trent Bridge should be taken by a Nottinghamshire bowler. Playing for England against India, Stuart Broad became the 12th Englishman and 39th overall to take three wickets in three balls at the highest level of the game. He had MS Dhoni caught at slip by James Anderson, Harbhajan Singh trapped lbw in his crease and then a full, swinging delivery crashed into Praveen Kumar's stumps. Broad's stunning performance came during a spell of 5.1-2-5-5 which deservedly earned him the man of the match honours in England's success.

THURSDAY 31st JULY 1884

There wouldn't have been much doubt about the winner of the man of the match award had one been available when Nottinghamshire hosted Gloucestershire at Trent Bridge. In one of the most staggering bowling performances in the history of county cricket, Alfred Shaw took a hat-trick in both innings and compounded his dominance with a further three wickets in four balls in the first innings. Shaw took a total of 14 wickets in the match, conceding 65 runs in 79 overs.

SATURDAY 31st JULY 1976

Scoring Nottinghamshire's highest individual score in 24 years, Derek Randall made 204 on the opening day of a championship match against Somerset at Trent Bridge. Sadly for the Retford-born batsman, the outcome of the contest failed to make it a milestone worth celebrating. Chasing 301 to win on the final day, the visitors romped to a six-wicket win thanks to a stunning maiden century from Ian Botham. The 20-year-old, showing an early glimpse of the form which would typify much of his career, blazed his way to 167 not out, with 20 boundaries and six maximums.

FRIDAY 31st JULY 1981

Showing that sportsmanship was still alive and well in the first-class game, Derek Randall was given a reprieve on the way to scoring a century. At Hinckley, against Leicestershire, bowler Chris Balderstone felt that the enthusiastic batsman was backing up too far, too quickly. Instead of delivering the ball, the bowler whipped off a bail. Initially given out, "Rags" was recalled by the home skipper Roger Tolchard and went on to make 101 in a match eventually won by Leicestershire.

NOTTINGHAMSHIRE CCC
On This Day

AUGUST

SUNDAY 1st AUGUST 1971

Incredibly, Garfield Sobers only scored one List A century during his career. That came in a John Player League match at Newark, for Nottinghamshire against Worcestershire. The visitors made 202-9 but thanks to an unbeaten 116 from their inspirational captain, Notts completed a six-wicket victory.

SUNDAY 1st AUGUST 2004

Between August 1980 and August 2004, Nottinghamshire played four first-class and six List A fixtures at the Sports Ground in Cleethorpes. Only Tim Robinson, Mick Newell and Jason Gallian scored hundreds for the home county during that period but the highest individual innings came from Durham's Marcus North, who hit 121 not out in his side's six-wicket victory in the final contest there.

MONDAY 1st AUGUST 2011

Performing the role of substitute fielder, in a Test on your home ground, would be an understandably daunting experience for any young cricketer. Fielding for England at Trent Bridge, against India, 21-year-old Nottinghamshire all-rounder Scott Elstone rose to the occasion in spectacular fashion by holding on to two pressure-laden catches in the deep, dismissing Suresh Raina and Harbhajan Singh from the bowling of Tim Bresnan.

TUESDAY 2nd AUGUST 1977

Derek Randall savoured the experience of hitting the winning runs at his home ground when he took England over the finishing line against Australia at Trent Bridge. The Nottinghamshire batsman had been involved in an unfortunate run out in the first innings but had the satisfaction of being there at the end, making 19 not out, to guide his side to their seven-wicket triumph.

TUESDAY 2nd AUGUST 2011

Unusually, both of Nottinghamshire's opening batsmen for their county championship match against Durham at Chester-le-Street were making their first-class debuts. Sam Kelsall, an 18-year-old right-hander who had been born in Stoke-on-Trent, made scores of 11 and 4, whilst his partner Karl Turner reached 9 and 40. The left-handed Turner, 23, hailed from Durham and had been released by his home county without making an appearance.

SATURDAY 3rd AUGUST 1974

The Rutland Recreation Ground in Ilkeston was the scene for one of Garfield Sobers' more explosive innings for Nottinghamshire. The West Indian blazed his way to a quick-fire 130 against Derbyshire, the hundred coming in just 83 minutes. His innings earned Sobers the Walter Lawrence Trophy for the fastest century of the season.

WEDNESDAY 4th AUGUST 2010

In his 100th first-class innings for Nottinghamshire, David Hussey scored an unbeaten 251 against Yorkshire at Headingley. It was the 22nd century, and third double-hundred, he had scored for Notts. The Australian's liking for the ground was obvious, this innings taking his career record at Leeds to a total of 832 runs from just eight knocks, at an average of 138.66.

TUESDAY 5th AUGUST 1969

Vasbert Drakes spent one season with Nottinghamshire, 1999, but he certainly made his mark. In 17 first-class matches he scored 427 runs at 15.81, with a top score of 80 versus Kent at Trent Bridge. Quick enough to be labelled a genuine fast bowler, he took 80 wickets at 22.42, with a best of 6-39. In 16 List A matches he also scored 188 runs and claimed 27 victims. Born in Barbados, Drakes features in *Wisden* as one of only four batsmen to have ever been given timed out. Scheduled to appear for Border against Free State in September 2002 his flight was delayed by several hours and he didn't arrive in time to bat in the first innings.

FRIDAY 6th AUGUST 1937

Chasing a target of 310 in just three hours is always a little daunting. However, playing against Kent at Canterbury, Nottinghamshire cantered to a five-wicket success, achieved with a full 45 minutes to spare. Joe Hardstaff junior was the architect behind the win, rattling up a century in just 51 minutes, an innings that won him the Walter Lawrence Trophy for the fastest of the summer. After arriving at the crease he scored 117 out of 134 runs added in an hour and although he fell for 126, the victory was already well within sight.

SUNDAY 7th AUGUST 2011

A noisy and passionate crowd of 12,070 saw Nottinghamshire Outlaws bow out of the Twenty20 Cup, losing their home quarter-final against Somerset. The Outlaws made 169-5 and appeared on course for a place at Finals Day until a brutal stand of 66, in just 4.2 overs, between Kieron Pollard (47 not out) and Jos Buttler (34 not out) saw the visitors through by six wickets.

SUNDAY 8th AUGUST 1909

One of the two Nottinghamshire bowlers who became embroiled in the "leg-theory" controversy of the 1930s, William "Bill" Voce was born in Annesley Woodhouse. Having originally started as a left-arm spin bowler, he developed greater speed, in-swing and, on responsive wickets, an unplayable leg-break, to become one of the best of his generation. For England, he took 98 wickets at 27.88, from 27 Tests but his county figures are quite staggering. Between 1927 and 1952 he made 345 appearances for Notts, taking 1,312 wickets at 22.26 with a best of 8-30. His batting performances brought him 6,398 runs at an average of 19.86. He scored four centuries, a best of 129 coming against Glamorgan at Trent Bridge in 1931.

SUNDAY 8th AUGUST 1982

Richard Hadlee scored two Test and 12 other first-class hundreds but his only one-day century came for Nottinghamshire. Promoted to number three in the order, the left-hander made 100 not out, in a John Player League match against Gloucestershire at the College Ground, Cheltenham. His runs helped post a total of 214-6 from the allotted 40 overs, with the Kiwi all-rounder then taking 2-33 in the 47-run victory.

MONDAY 9th AUGUST 1847

Henry Attenburrow is credited with being the only Nottinghamshire bowler to take ten wickets in his debut match for the county. At Trent Bridge, against England in a three-day match, Attenburrow took four in the first innings and six more in the second. His complete analysis has not been recorded but the match constituted half of his entire first-class career as he only played once more for the county, taking a further five wickets against Sheffield.

MONDAY 9th AUGUST 1847

Apart from the achievements of Henry Attenburrow, the match against England at Trent Bridge saw another record set which has stood unchallenged ever since. Making his debut was Southwell-born Robert Crispin "Cris" Tinley. Aged just 16 years and 288 days, he remains Nottinghamshire's youngest first-class cricketer. Tinley collected three-wicket hauls in each innings but didn't appear again until July 1848.

THURSDAY 9th AUGUST 1917

Medium-slow left-arm bowler William Riley made 80 first-class appearances for Nottinghamshire, picking up 235 wickets at an average of 23.39. His best performance was the 7-80 he took against Leicestershire at Trent Bridge in 1911. That same season he was the fortunate batsman to be at the non-striker's end and witness Ted Alletson's sustained assault against Sussex at Hove. The pair added 152 for the last wicket, with Riley's share an unbeaten ten. Gunner Riley was killed by a shell splinter in Belgium, two days short of his 29th birthday.

THURSDAY 10th AUGUST 1978

Paignton in Devon was the birthplace of Christopher Mark Wells Read, who made his Nottinghamshire debut in 1998. The wicketkeeper/batsman immediately became a Trent Bridge favourite and made his Test debut just 14 months later. His first century, 160 against Warwickshire, also came in 1999, and over the next decade he established himself as one of the very best in his profession. Adjudged unfortunate not to have made more than 15 Test and 36 ODI appearances, England's loss became Nottinghamshire's gain as Read assumed the county captaincy in 2008, leading his side to the championship title two years later.

MONDAY 10th AUGUST 1987

Richard Hadlee became the first Nottinghamshire player since John Gunn in 1921 to score a hundred and take ten wickets in a match at Trent Bridge. The New Zealand Test all-rounder scored 101, either side of figures of 6-42 and 6-41. Fittingly, he was there at the crease with 23 not out in his second innings as Notts crept over the winning line to secure a five-wicket success.

MONDAY 11th AUGUST 1884

In a draw at the Kennington Oval, Nottinghamshire's William Scotton scored 90 in England's first innings, his highest international score. Earlier, in Australia's 551, Scotton's only bowl in Test cricket cost 20 runs from five overs but was significant in that all 11 members of the fielding side bowled, the first time this had happened in Test cricket.

SATURDAY 11th AUGUST 1928

Two former Nottinghamshire cricketers made their debuts as Test match umpires on the same day. Joe Hardstaff senior, who had made 340 appearances for the county, and Thomas Oates, who had played in 420 matches, stood together in the England v West Indies Test at The Oval. Perhaps fittingly, the first wicket of the contest was taken by Harold Larwood, the only other Notts man participating. Hardstaff stood in a total of 21 Tests, including two at Trent Bridge.

SATURDAY 11th AUGUST 1990

Vivian Richards' highest individual score against Nottinghamshire came on an amazing day of cricket at Worksop. In his first season with Glamorgan, the West Indian scored a mighty seven centuries, with his innings of 127 at the Town Ground as exciting as any of them. His runs came from just 136 deliveries, with 14 fours and five sixes. Hugh Morris and Matthew Maynard also scored hundreds as the Welsh county reached 427. With just one over left in the day, there was still time for an unusual occurrence, as Notts promoted Andy Pick from the number nine position, to open the batting and see out the session as night-watchman.

SATURDAY 12th AUGUST 1905

Any record that lasts for more than a century is worthy of praise. Although the final day of Nottinghamshire's clash with Essex at Leyton was allowed to peter out into a tame draw, it did enable Arthur Jones and John Gunn to spend time in the middle getting to know each other a little better. Opener Jones made 274 and Gunn reached 151 as a new county record fourth-wicket stand of 361 was posted.

TWO OF NOTTINGHAMSHIRE'S AUSTRALIANS, DAVID HUSSEY (LEFT) WITH ADAM VOGES

SATURDAY 12th AUGUST 2006

Twenty20 Finals Day at Trent Bridge didn't go how the home supporters hoped. Nottinghamshire Outlaws' first participation at Finals Day saw them outclass Surrey in the semi-final to set up a showdown with Leicestershire Foxes in the final. Batting first, the Foxes made 177-2 but the Outlaws came agonisingly close to their target before falling four runs short. There was a feeling that they were perhaps a little hard done by, with the final ball of the contest appearing to be above waist height before it was whacked over the ropes for six by Will Smith. Despite being under pressure from the crowd to award a no-ball, the umpires called time, both on the contest and on Notts' hopes.

THURSDAY 13th AUGUST 1959

No other wicketkeeper in Nottinghamshire's history has taken as many catches as the 737 held by Bruce Nicholas French, who made 324 appearances for the county between 1976 and 1995. Only by virtue of having taken fewer stumpings than Thomas Oates, he stands as second on the county list of wicketkeeper dismissals, with a total of 829. Born in Warsop, French made two first-class centuries for Notts and played 16 Tests for England.

MONDAY 13th AUGUST 1984

The highest score by Richard Hadlee during his 342 first-class matches came at Lord's when he reached 210 not out for Nottinghamshire against Middlesex. He had come to the crease with his side in strife, at 17-4, and produced a master-class, from 261 deliveries faced. He batted for 356 minutes, scoring 24 fours and one six. Turning the game on its head, Notts won by an innings, Kevin Cooper taking career-best figures of 8-44 in Middlesex's second effort.

TUESDAY 13th AUGUST 2002

Nottinghamshire's Bilal Shafayat enjoyed the finest of matches whilst representing England Under-19s against their Indian counterparts in a Youth Test at Northampton. The right-handed batsman followed up his first-innings 118 by making an unbeaten 201 in the second. Alongside Shafayat in England's victory were county team-mates Samit Patel and Paul McMahon.

SATURDAY 14th AUGUST 1897

WG Grace became the first (and so far only) cricketer to score a century and take five wickets in a match against Nottinghamshire for a second time. At the College Ground, Cheltenham, he took 6-36 after scoring 131, emulating his feat of 21 years earlier when he scored 177 and took 8-69 at the Clifton College Close Ground. Not surprisingly Gloucestershire won both matches.

THURSDAY 14th AUGUST 1980

Kevin Cooper's only senior representative call-up came with an appearance for Young England against Australia at New Road, Worcester. The Nottinghamshire seamer trapped Aussie skipper Greg Chappell in an 11-over spell which cost 48 runs. Replying to a score of 176-4, Young England had lost Notts opener Tim Robinson for seven when rain wiped out the remainder of the contest.

SATURDAY 14th AUGUST 2010

Nottinghamshire Outlaws fell at the semi-final stage on Twenty20 Finals Day at The Rose Bowl, Southampton. In a weather-interrupted match, Notts were on 117-4 when rain brought a premature conclusion to their innings, leaving Somerset victors by three runs under Duckworth/Lewis calculations. Earlier, the south-west county had made 182-5, which seemed within reach until Samit Patel was brilliantly taken high above his head, on the long-on boundary, by Kieron Pollard for 39. Moments later, the umpires called off the contest.

FRIDAY 15th AUGUST 1930

After 20 years of service to Nottinghamshire, William "Dodger" Whysall's 50th and final century for the county was also his largest. Playing against Northamptonshire at Trent Bridge the 42-year-old opener scored 248, an innings which also took him past 2,000 runs for a fifth consecutive season.

WEDNESDAY 15th AUGUST 1956

On 75 separate occasions leg-spinner Bruce Dooland took five wickets or more in an innings for Nottinghamshire. His best return was at Trent Bridge against Worcestershire, when his figures read 19-14-20-8. In the second innings he bamboozled them for a second time, collecting 5-59.

MONDAY 15th AUGUST 1977

To win the Ashes is often the crowning moment of any English Test cricketer's career. Nottinghamshire's Derek Randall was able to bring about that moment himself, catching Australia's Rod Marsh at Headingley to take his side to an unassailable 3-0 lead in the series.

WEDNESDAY 16th AUGUST 1905

Arthur Jones, on his 33rd birthday, became the first substitute fielder to keep wicket in a Test. The Nottinghamshire batsman, who played a dozen Tests, stood in for the injured Dick Lilley and took a catch at The Oval to dismiss Australia's Warwick Armstrong.

TUESDAY 16th AUGUST 1977

Basharat "Basher" Hassan scored 15 first-class centuries for Nottinghamshire during two decades with the county. The highest score made by the right-hander came in 1977, when he hit 182 not out against Gloucestershire at Trent Bridge.

FRIDAY 16th AUGUST 2002

Having picked up five wickets on his first appearance for Nottinghamshire, at Worcestershire a week before, Australian leg-spinner Stuart MacGill turned in a sensational performance on his Trent Bridge debut for the county. His first-innings analysis of 8-111 was followed by 6-54 in the second, as Middlesex were spun to defeat by an innings and 73 runs.

THURSDAY 17th AUGUST 1916

Eric Alfred Meads was a wicketkeeper who had made one appearance for Nottinghamshire before the start of the Second World War. Born in Carrington, he retained his place when county cricket re-started in 1946 and went on to make 205 appearances for the Trent Bridge side. He was involved in 446 dismissals behind the stumps and twice took six catches in an innings.

WEDNESDAY 17th AUGUST 1966

Before the start of a championship match at Trent Bridge against Leicestershire, Mike Smedley was awarded his Nottinghamshire county cap by skipper Norman Hill. The right-handed batsman promptly celebrated by scoring 134 not out, his second career century, in a drawn contest.

MONDAY 18th AUGUST 2008

Nottinghamshire's Samit Patel made his England debut in an ODI against Scotland at The Grange, Edinburgh. He took 1-22 but wasn't required to bat after rain caused an early abandonment.

SUNDAY 19th AUGUST 1951

Nirmal Nanan was a right-handed batsman and a leg-break and googly bowler who featured for Nottinghamshire during the early 1970s. Hailing from Trinidad and Tobago, he moved to England and made his Notts debut against Oxford University at The Parks, scoring 72 and taking 3-12, performances that would ultimately prove to be his best figures for the county. Over the next decade he made just 32 first-class appearances, scoring just 846 runs. He also played in 32 one-day matches for Nottinghamshire and, perhaps fittingly, saved his finest performance for his final match. Playing in a Benson and Hedges Cup match against Derbyshire at Trent Bridge, he opened the batting and was eventually run out for 93 in a huge win, earning himself the man of the match award.

MONDAY 19th AUGUST 1957

Australian Bruce Dooland scored his only century for Nottinghamshire against Sussex at Worthing. His unbeaten 115 proved to be the highest score of his 214-match career.

SATURDAY 19th AUGUST 1978

Nottingham-born David Lucas was a left-arm medium-fast bowler who represented his home county between 1999 and 2002. He took 52 wickets in 22 first-class appearances, with a best of 5-104. His career then took him to Northamptonshire, before signing for Worcestershire ahead of the 2012 season.

SUNDAY 19th AUGUST 1979

The only time that Nottinghamshire have recorded a last-wicket partnership of 50 in a List A match came at Northampton in a losing cause. The home side scored 150-5 from their 40 overs in a John Player League match. Nottinghamshire were out of it at 94-9 but Eddie Hemmings, with 43 not out, and Mike Bore, who made an undefeated 28, nearly got them to the winning line as the innings closed on 144-9.

TUESDAY 19th AUGUST 2008

Temporary floodlights had been in use at many grounds since the advent of day/night cricket a decade earlier. Trent Bridge's first permanent lights were built by Abacus Lighting of Sutton-in-Ashfield. The lights, on top of six 40-metre high masts, were first used for a Pro40 defeat against Durham.

WEDNESDAY 20th AUGUST 1958

Gamini Goonesena had a match to remember for Nottinghamshire against Leicestershire at Grace Road. The leg-break and googly bowler, who had been born in Colombo, Ceylon (now Sri Lanka), followed up his first-innings figures of 11-4-19-6 with a best for the county analysis of 27-4-63-7. Goonesena took 299 wickets for Notts in just 94 matches, although his career-best figures of 8-39 came as a student, for Cambridge University.

SATURDAY 20th AUGUST 1977

Many visiting captains have elected to field first when winning the toss ahead of a championship game at Trent Bridge – and Surrey's Robin Jackman may wish he'd done the same. After a rain delay, his troops were out for just 79 on the opening day, with Clive Rice prominent, taking 6-29 from his 13.2 overs. Despite their early advantage, more bad weather prevented Notts from being able to get more than a draw out of the game.

THURSDAY 20th AUGUST 1987

Nottinghamshire had four representatives selected in the match arranged to celebrate the bicentenary of Marylebone Cricket Club. Playing for MCC against a Rest of the World XI in a five-day unofficial Test at Lord's were Chris Broad, Clive Rice, Richard Hadlee and Bruce French. The match ended in a draw, Rice's undefeated 59 the leading contribution from the Trent Bridge quartet.

SATURDAY 21st AUGUST 1976

Ahead of Nottinghamshire's championship match against Sussex at Hove, Clive Rice's highest first-class score had been just 113. Putting that right in a spectacular manner, the South African compiled a majestic 246, the fourth of his 37 hundreds for the county.

MONDAY 21st AUGUST 1989

The second morning against Derbyshire at Trent Bridge began with 20 wickets having already gone down on the Saturday. With a 20-run advantage Nottinghamshire began again but both openers, Chris Broad and Paul Pollard, were struck whilst batting. At the fall of Broad's wicket – at 11.40am – the umpires left the field to telephone the TCCB and ask for guidance. After a two-hour delay, play re-started on another wicket, the one used for the recent Test match. Derbyshire's West Indian fast bowler Michael Holding disagreed with the decision and took no further part in the contest. Wickets continued to fall steadily – Notts all out for 114 and Derbyshire folding for just 64 in their second innings. Despite the 70-run victory, Nottinghamshire were docked 25 points for preparing an unsatisfactory surface.

FRIDAY 22nd AUGUST 1997

New Zealand Test player Nathan Astle made ten first-class appearances for Nottinghamshire, scoring 644 runs at an average of 40.25. He scored two centuries, both finishing on exactly 100. His first had come against Warwickshire at Trent Bridge, before adding a second on this day at Worksop against Essex. The Kiwi added 193 for the second wicket with Tim Robinson, who made 143.

WEDNESDAY 22nd AUGUST 2007

Mark Davies' Nottinghamshire career was brief but effective. The new-ball bowler was signed on a short-term loan from parent club Durham but played only one match, at Trent Bridge against Northamptonshire. Bettering anything he'd previously produced in 50 matches for his home county, Davies took 7-59 and later 1-31 in Notts' victory, as well as adding an unbeaten 35, his second-best score.

THURSDAY 23rd AUGUST 1951

Medium-pace bowler Philip Wilkinson was born in Hucknall and represented Notts between 1971 and 1977. He played 92 matches, taking 175 wickets, with a best of 6-81. Although not particularly renowned for his batting, he also made two half-centuries, with a top score of 77. A broken leg, sustained whilst playing football, set back his progress and he announced his retirement when many felt he still had much to offer.

FRIDAY 24th AUGUST 1973

Garfield Sobers' 26th and final Test century was one of his most stylish but came in two parts. Caressing the ball around the Lord's outfield he scored an unbeaten 132 before retiring due to a stomach upset. He later returned to reach 150 not out, as the West Indies declared on 652-8 against England. Altogether, Sobers batted for 288 minutes, faced 277 deliveries and hit 19 fours. Rohan Kanhai and Bernard Julien also scored centuries on the way to a convincing Test victory.

MONDAY 25th AUGUST 1856

William Clarke was 57 when he died at his home, Priory Lodge, at Wandsworth, Surrey. He had prospered greatly from the game of cricket, having developed the meadow at the back of the Trent Bridge Inn for use as the new headquarters of the county side. Despite losing an eye in the late 1820s, after being hit by a fives ball, Clarke had gone on to play 143 first-class matches, taking approximately 797 wickets with his underarm spin bowling. He helped set up the All England Eleven, a touring side made up of the best players in the country. This venture had proved extremely profitable for Clarke, who then moved to London, leaving Trent Bridge in the hands of his stepson, John Chapman. Clarke's activities with the All England Eleven reduced the number of appearances for Nottinghamshire to a trickle, his last outing against England in August 1855 aged 56 years and eight months, the oldest player ever to represent the county. Clarke was survived by his son, Alfred, who also played for Nottinghamshire. In 1990, a stand at Trent Bridge was named after William Clarke, in his honour.

SUNDAY 25th AUGUST 1991

A nine-wicket win over Derbyshire, at Trent Bridge, secured Notts their first one-day league title. Needing to beat their local rivals to make sure of finishing ahead of Lancashire, they restricted their opponents to 176-9 from their allotted 40 overs. Despite losing Derek Randall for 67, with the score on 134, an unbeaten 73 from Chris Broad and 25 not out from captain Tim Robinson saw Nottinghamshire to their 13th win out of 16 matches and a deserved evening of celebrations.

STUART BROAD TOOK TRENT BRIDGE'S FIRST TEST MATCH HAT-TRICK IN 2011

THURSDAY 26th AUGUST 1993

Mathew Peter "Matt" Dowman, playing for England's Under-19s against their West Indian counterparts at Hove, scored 267. Amongst his team-mates were future Test batsmen Michael Vaughan and Marcus Trescothick, whilst the opposition included Shivnarine Chanderpaul. Earlier in the month Dowman had made his Nottinghamshire debut against Yorkshire in the AXA Equity and Law League.

SUNDAY 26th AUGUST 2007

An outstanding all-round performance from Graeme Swann inspired Nottinghamshire Outlaws to a convincing win in the Pro40 League over Gloucestershire Gladiators. His swashbuckling 59 from 33 deliveries was followed by an almost unplayable spell of eight overs which returned figures of 5-17. A crowd of 4,000 witnessed the performance, which was immediately followed by the start of extensive ground redevelopments. The two-tier Parr Stand, built in 1955, and named after the mid-19th-century batsman, was demolished to make way for a new, larger stand and administrative centre.

TUESDAY 26th AUGUST 2008

Putting on a show in front of your own fans is always the goal for any England player. When Stuart Broad faced South Africa in a one-day international at Trent Bridge, he excelled to the tune of 5-23, his first five-wicket haul in ODIs. Bowled out for just 83 in only 23 overs, the South Africans were booed from the field, although they had no answer to the Nottinghamshire paceman who was helped by four catches from wicketkeeper Matt Prior, who took six in total and then scored an unbeaten 45 in England's ten-wicket win.

WEDNESDAY 27th AUGUST 1969

Born near Ashford, in Kent, Mark Alan Ealham followed his father, Alan Ealham, in playing for the county of his birth, making 173 first-class and 260 List A appearances for them, as well as representing England in eight Tests and 64 one-day internationals. Switching counties, Ealham joined Nottinghamshire in 2004 and helped them win the county championship a year later. By the time of his retirement at the end of the 2009 campaign, the all-rounder had appeared in 89 first-class, 75 one-day and 47 Twenty20 matches for the Trent Bridge side.

TUESDAY 27th AUGUST 1974

Garfield Sobers' final home championship match for Nottinghamshire ended in a draw against Derbyshire at Trent Bridge. During the lunch interval he was presented with a silver tankard by the club president, Frank Gregory. It was inscribed "To Gary Sobers – a great player and a gentleman".

FRIDAY 27th AUGUST 2010

Stuart Broad's recognition as a fully-fledged Test all-rounder was made complete after his maiden century at the highest level. Against Pakistan at Lord's, the Nottinghamshire quick bowler put on an exhibition of high-quality strokeplay to score 169, made from 297 deliveries faced and with 18 fours and a six. Although the legitimacy of Broad's century is beyond doubt, the aftermath of the contest saw three Pakistan players face custodial sentences after being found guilty of spot-fixing offences during the Test.

FRIDAY 27th AUGUST 2010

Whilst Stuart Broad (see above) was shining for England, Nottinghamshire were pulling off a stunning three-wicket win over Lancashire at Trent Bridge. The day contained a unique occurrence in first-class cricket with opening batsman Alex Hales dismissed twice in the 90s. The morning began with him on 87 but he soon fell for 98 to Kyle Hogg. After two declarations, Nottinghamshire were batting again after lunch, chasing 260, which they achieved with Hales again in dominating form before losing his wicket to Gary Keedy, for 93.

MONDAY 28th AUGUST 1995

Nottinghamshire created some unwanted history at the end of a quite extraordinary match. Never, in the history of the game, has a side scored as many as 527 runs – and still lost by an innings! Tim Robinson's 209 and 158 from Graeme Archer (the pair added 294 for the second wicket) took Notts to a seemingly invincible position. That was proved incorrect, however, as four centurions saw Northants through to 781-7 declared, their highest-ever total. Beginning the final day 254 behind, Notts looked to bat through the day for a draw but lost wickets steadily – the final one falling with just 17 deliveries remaining, to lose by an innings and 97.

MONDAY 28th AUGUST 2006

Chris Read made one Twenty20 appearance for England. The Nottinghamshire wicketkeeper played against Pakistan at Bristol and scored 13 from 11 deliveries in 144-7. Responding, the tourists reached their target with five wickets and 13 deliveries remaining. The glove-man took one catch, Younis Khan, who had briefly been a Trent Bridge team-mate in 2005.

SUNDAY 29th AUGUST 1993

Nottinghamshire posted their highest ever List A score, 329-6, in an AXA Equity and Law League match against Derbyshire at Trent Bridge. Batting first, the home side were indebted to scores of 91 from Paul Pollard, an unbeaten 78 from Tim Robinson and 75 from Paul Johnson to help them to their record total. Derbyshire were then dismissed for just 187, leaving Notts winners by 142 runs.

SUNDAY 29th AUGUST 1999

Vasbert Drakes' most startling performance for Nottinghamshire came in a match that had been virtually conceded. Playing against Derbyshire at Trent Bridge, in the 45-overs-a-side CGU National League, the home side mustered 269-7. Nevertheless, it didn't look like being enough as the visitors began the final over on 260-5, requiring just ten runs to win. To everyone's sheer astonishment, the West Indian fast bowler then produced a once-in-a-lifetime finish. He yorked Phil DeFreitas with the first ball and then removed Adrian Rollins' middle stump with the next. He needed the assistance of the umpire to get his hat-trick – James Pyemont palpably out lbw – and then, for good measure, a full-length delivery took out the leg stump of Simon Lacey. Four wickets in four balls – the only time it has happened for a Nottinghamshire bowler in the shortened format of the game. A dot ball and a single ended the over by the way, enabling Notts to defeat their closest rivals in the most dramatic fashion imaginable.

THURSDAY 29th AUGUST 2002

South African Test bowler Nicky Boje made nine championship appearances for Nottinghamshire, taking a total of 27 wickets. His best performance was saved until last, the spinner returning 6-128 from 42 overs against Glamorgan at Colwyn Bay.

FRIDAY 29th AUGUST 2008

In just his fourth ODI for England, Samit Patel collected his first five-wicket haul. Playing at The Oval against South Africa, the Nottinghamshire all-rounder returned figures of 5-41. Having earlier scored 31 from 33 deliveries his contributions had proved significant in England's 126-run victory.

SATURDAY 29th AUGUST 2009

There's nothing like the television cameras to bring out the best in a player. In a live televised NatWest Pro40 League fixture against Worcestershire at Trent Bridge, Nottinghamshire's Alex Hales blasted an unbeaten 150, from just 102 balls, with 13 fours and eight sixes. The 20-year-old right-hander had put on a special show for the viewers, although a century from Steven Davies and 87 not out from Steve Moore took Worcestershire to their target of 283 and spoiled the day somewhat.

MONDAY 29th AUGUST 2011

The end of a player's career is always an emotional occasion, especially for someone who has been in the professional game for more than two decades. Forty-one-year-old Ali Brown bowed out of county cricket after playing in a Clydesdale Bank 40 match at Trent Bridge against Lancashire. Notts didn't win but the day was still a memorable one for the former Surrey and England batsman, who said afterwards: "I've never had a standing ovation for scoring just 18 before!"

THURSDAY 30th AUGUST 1984

Northamptonshire were spun to a crushing defeat inside two days at Trent Bridge. Slow left-arm bowler Mike Bore claimed match figures of 9-124, with off-spinner Eddie Hemmings collecting 8-152 in the match, including a hat-trick in the second innings.

TUESDAY 30th AUGUST 1994

The highest score of Graeme Archer's first-class career was the 168 he made for Nottinghamshire against Glamorgan at Worksop. His runs, plus 99 from Tim Robinson, saw the side to a first-innings total of 476-6 declared, enough to win the match by an innings and 37 runs.

SATURDAY 31st AUGUST 1968

This was the record-breaking day when Garfield Sobers re-wrote cricket history. The Nottinghamshire captain arrived at the crease, against Glamorgan at Swansea, with his side on 308-5 and in need of quick runs before a declaration. Facing Malcolm Nash, a 23-year-old who had opened the bowling with his left-arm medium-pacers before switching to spin, Sobers became the first batsman to score 36 runs from an over by hitting all six deliveries for six.

SATURDAY 31st AUGUST 1974

Trent Bridge staged its first one-day international, with England losing to Pakistan in a rain-reduced match. Lancashire's David Lloyd, later to become England coach and a well-respected journalist and broadcaster, had the honour of scoring the first ODI century on the ground but he was quickly followed to the landmark by Pakistan's Majid Khan who steered his side to a seven-wicket triumph.

NOTTINGHAMSHIRE CCC
On This Day

SEPTEMBER

THURSDAY 1st SEPTEMBER 1927

Nottinghamshire began their second innings against Glamorgan knowing a draw would be enough to secure the county title. Having won 12 matches already and against a side that hadn't tasted victory throughout 1927, Notts were understandably confident of returning home in celebration and a civic reception had already been prepared. Little did they realise, when they advanced to 23-2 at the close, they would be bustled out for 61 the following morning to lose by an innings – which saw Lancashire pip them to the crown by just two points.

FRIDAY 2nd SEPTEMBER 1977

Clive Rice's best bowling analysis for Nottinghamshire came at New Road against Worcestershire. In a rain-interrupted match, the home side were set 240 in two and three-quarter hours on the final day. Hopes of getting anywhere near were quickly dispelled as Rice picked up the wickets of Barry Jones, Gordon Wilcock and Ted Hemsley in the first over, which ended with the score 0-3. It was soon 14-5 and eventually 89 all out, with Rice's figures reading 11.5-4-16-6. Nottinghamshire's victory celebrations were understandable – it was their first win of the season, at the 21st attempt!

MONDAY 2nd SEPTEMBER 1985

With 8-41, Richard Hadlee's best figures for Nottinghamshire came against Lancashire at Trent Bridge. The match ended in a draw after the visitors had been set 199 in 39 overs but a spell of 6-51 from Eddie Hemmings forced the Red Rose county to abandon a victory push and bat out time.

THURSDAY 2nd SEPTEMBER 1993

The only first-class match to be played at Ropery Lane, Chester-le-Street, certainly met with the approval of Chris Lewis and Bruce French who both made the best scores of their careers. The Nottinghamshire duo set a new seventh-wicket record for the county as Durham subsided to defeat by an innings and 157 runs. Having been 4-2 at one stage, Notts turned it round to reach 629, with 130 from Paul Johnson, followed by 247 from Lewis and 123 from French, who combined in a stand of 301.

PAUL JOHNSON SCORED A RECORD 10,025 LIST-A RUNS FOR NOTTS

SUNDAY 3rd SEPTEMBER 2000

In knock-out competition the highest opening stand for Nottinghamshire is 199 by Mike Harris and Basharat Hassan against Yorkshire in 1973. Darren Bicknell and Jason Gallian came close to surpassing it with 196 against Surrey at Trent Bridge. Bicknell, against his former county, scored 115, with Gallian adding 84. The partnership was the highest by a Notts opening pair in any of the various formats of the Sunday League.

SATURDAY 4th SEPTEMBER 1971

Lance Klusener was born in Durban, South Africa. The international all-rounder joined Notts for a brief period during the 2002 season, playing one first-class match and five List A fixtures. His only championship outing brought him 42 runs and one wicket, whilst in limited-overs cricket he scored 144 runs for the county and collected four wickets.

SUNDAY 4th SEPTEMBER 1994

Bowling against Glamorgan in an AXA Equity and Law League match at Trent Bridge, Nottinghamshire's Kevin Evans claimed the only List A hat-trick of his career, dismissing Roland Lefebvre, Colin Metson and Steve Watkin in successive deliveries. All were clean bowled, as were Tony Cottey and Robert Croft earlier in the innings, Evans collecting match-winning figures of 5-29.

WEDNESDAY 5th SEPTEMBER 1973

Garfield Sobers failed to make his mark during the only ODI he appeared in. Playing for the West Indies, against England at Headingley, he was dismissed for 0 by Yorkshire's Chris Old. The 37-year-old Sobers, taking time out from his Nottinghamshire duties, got revenge of sorts later by bowling Old but England managed to win the match by just one wicket, with three balls to spare.

MONDAY 6th SEPTEMBER 1880

In the first Test match in England, the home side defeated Australia by five wickets at The Oval, with Nottinghamshire's Fred Morley taking eight wickets on debut including 5-56 in the first innings. WG Grace also played his maiden Test match and scored 152, the first instance of an England batsman scoring a Test century.

WEDNESDAY 6th SEPTEMBER 1995

A 60-run victory over Kent earned Nottinghamshire the Tetley Bitter Festival Trophy at Scarborough. Skippered by Paul Johnson, Notts made 197 with Chris Cairns hitting a lusty 62 not out. The reply soon ran into difficulties and only lasted 33.2 of the scheduled 40 overs.

WEDNESDAY 6th SEPTEMBER 2006

The first Nottinghamshire hat-trick of the 21st century was taken by Charlie Shreck. Playing at Lord's, against Middlesex, the Truro-born seamer dismissed Ed Smith, Eoin Morgan and Paul Weekes in consecutive deliveries during Notts' innings victory.

SUNDAY 7th SEPTEMBER 1980

A large Trent Bridge crowd turned out to pay their respects to Richard Hadlee, due to play his final match in Nottinghamshire colours. However, against Lancashire in the John Player League, he produced what would be the best one-day figures of his career, 6-12, to speed Notts to an easy victory. Inspired by the response from the supporters and team-mates, he went back on his decision to leave and agreed to return the following season.

SATURDAY 7th SEPTEMBER 1985

Nottinghamshire lost the final of the NatWest Trophy to Essex by just one run at Lord's. Seemingly out of it when they began the final over still requiring 18, Derek Randall had other ideas as he hit three balls for boundaries, and picked up four runs from the other two deliveries. Requiring only two from the final ball of the game, bowled by Derek Pringle, Randall chipped to mid-wicket, where Paul Prichard held the catch to shatter Nottinghamshire's dreams.

MONDAY 7th SEPTEMBER 1987

Nottinghamshire won the NatWest Trophy for the only time, defeating Northamptonshire in the final at Lord's by three wickets. The match had begun two days earlier, with the opposition making 228-3 from their 50 overs. Rain delays meant that the match was carried over until the Monday, Notts reaching their target thanks to 63 from skipper Clive Rice and an unbeaten 70, from 61 deliveries, by Richard Hadlee.

MONDAY 7th SEPTEMBER 2009

Although it's a bitter spill to swallow when it happens against you, Nottinghamshire's players were magnanimous in defeat as they succumbed to a sensational over from Sussex's Dwayne Smith in a NatWest Pro40 clash at Hove. The West Indian all-rounder bowled a four-wicket maiden, which included a hat-trick, as Notts' middle order crumbled to an eventual 152-run defeat. Bilal Shafayat, Kevin O'Brien and Jake Ball – on his county debut – fell in successive deliveries to the final three balls from Smith's third over, which had begun with the capture of Alex Hales' wicket. He had earlier removed Adam Voges and when Andrew Carter later fell, it brought the Barbadian his career-best figures of 6-29.

TUESDAY 7th SEPTEMBER 2010

Nottinghamshire fluffed their lines when facing Yorkshire at Trent Bridge. Entering their penultimate championship game of the season, the county knew that victory would secure them the title. Put in to bat, it all went horribly wrong though as they were humbled for just 59 in 33.2 overs. An extraordinary day, that saw 18 wickets fall, ended with visiting captain Andrew Gale unbeaten on 147 out of his side's 260-8.

MONDAY 8th SEPTEMBER 1980

Bruce Dooland was only 56 when he died at Bedford Park, near Adelaide in South Australia. The former Test match leg-spinner had spent five summers with Nottinghamshire, from 1953 to 1957, taking 770 wickets in 140 appearances and twice completed the double of 1,000 runs and 100 wickets in the same season.

THURSDAY 9th SEPTEMBER 1965

Arthur Staples died in Redhill, Nottinghamshire, aged 66. Having followed his elder brother Sam into the county team, Arthur made 358 first-class appearances between 1924 and 1938. A right-handed batsman, he scored 12,762 runs for Notts at an average of 28.17. The highest of his 12 centuries came against Cambridge University when he scored an unbeaten 153 at Fenners in 1936. A useful medium-pace bowler, he captured 635 wickets at 29.82, with a best of 7-20.

WEDNESDAY 9th SEPTEMBER 1998

The first floodlit match at Trent Bridge reached an unsatisfactory conclusion in every sense. Rain delayed the start until 7pm and then high winds prevented the temporary lights from being raised to their full height. On the field, in an AXA Equity and Law League match reduced to 26 overs per side, Lancashire made 221-2, with Andrew Flintoff clubbing an unbeaten 93 off 55 balls. Notts were then docked two overs for a sluggish performance in the field and could only make 169-4 in reply.

SUNDAY 10th SEPTEMBER 2000

Nottinghamshire Outlaws won promotion from the second division of the Norwich Union League after a tense three-run victory over Glamorgan Dragons at Trent Bridge. The home side made 229-9, with half-centuries from Paul Johnson and Usman Afzaal, before restricting their opponents to 226-9.

SATURDAY 10th SEPTEMBER 2011

Alex Hales, 22, carried his bat for an unbeaten century as Nottinghamshire fell to an innings defeat against Warwickshire at Edgbaston. The right-handed opening batsman followed his first-innings score of 72 with an undefeated 102 in his side's total of 222 all out.

TUESDAY 11th SEPTEMBER 1984

With the county championship at stake Richard Ollis, on the field as a substitute, broke Nottinghamshire hearts when he caught Mike Bore off the penultimate ball of a match against Somerset at Taunton. Chasing 297 to win and pip Essex for the crown, the visitors had brought the equation down to 14 from the final over and then four from the last two deliveries. Bore swung hard and handsome but couldn't clear Ollis on the long-off fence.

FRIDAY 11th SEPTEMBER 1987

Completing a fairytale week, which had begun with the lifting of the NatWest Trophy, Nottinghamshire collected the county championship title when they defeated Glamorgan at Trent Bridge. A century from Clive Rice and a six-wicket haul from Richard Hadlee set up the nine-wicket success to confirm a four-point victory over runners-up Lancashire.

SUNDAY 11th SEPTEMBER 1988

The largest of Derek Randall's 52 first-class centuries came at Trent Bridge against Derbyshire. Sharing in a fourth-wicket stand of 345 with Mick Newell, who made 105, the former England batsman scored 237, the third and final double century of his career. Nottinghamshire went on to make 614, winning by an innings and 41 runs.

SATURDAY 11th SEPTEMBER 1999

Nottinghamshire announced the signing of Pakistan fast bowler Shoaib Akhtar as their overseas player for 2000. Akhtar arrived at Trent Bridge the following May carrying a rib injury sustained whilst playing for his country in Sharjah. The injury didn't respond to treatment quickly enough and the county were forced to replace Akhtar with Paul Reiffel of Australia.

MONDAY 12th SEPTEMBER 2011

Nottinghamshire's second string won the Second Eleven Trophy for the first time since 1991, by defeating Lancashire at Liverpool by four wickets. Chasing an all-out total of 192, Notts were sent on their way by an innings of 49 from Neil Edwards before the captain, Scott Elstone, saw his side over the finishing line with a run-a-ball 69.

THURSDAY 13th SEPTEMBER 1917

Charles Pepper was killed in action at the Battle of Passchendaele, aged 42. Born in County Cork, the Irish youngster played seven first-class matches for Notts, scoring 162 runs, with a top score of 40 not out. He also picked up three wickets, all in a spell of 3-23 against Essex at Leyton in 1901. A former sergeant in the Sherwood Foresters, Pepper's body is buried at the La Clytte Military Cemetery in Klijte, Belgium.

SATURDAY 13th SEPTEMBER 2003

Russell Warren scored five centuries for Nottinghamshire in 36 first-class matches, with two coming in the same fixture. Against Middlesex at Lord's, he made 123 in the first innings and an unbeaten 113 in the second, to become only the 19th different player to achieve the feat for the county.

MONDAY 14th SEPTEMBER 1981

Amidst scenes of great jubilation Nottinghamshire completed a two-day victory over Glamorgan at Trent Bridge to clinch the county championship for the first time in 52 years. Home nerves had already been eased on the first morning when the Welsh side were dismissed for just 60 – Richard Hadlee's 4-18 taking him past 100 wickets for the season. Notts only made 180 themselves but then dismissed Glamorgan again quickly, leaving only 30 required before the champagne corks began popping.

FRIDAY 14th SEPTEMBER 1990

Despite it being in a losing cause, Chris Broad's 122 for Notts against Lancashire at Trent Bridge enabled him to equal a county record. His ninth century of the season matched the feat of WW Whysall in 1928 and MJ Harris in 1971.

SUNDAY 14th SEPTEMBER 2008

In one of the best one-day innings ever seen at Trent Bridge, Sussex's Murray Goodwin cruelly denied Nottinghamshire the silverware they appeared to have at least one hand on. In a straight winner-takes-all shoot-out to decide who would win the NatWest Pro40 League, the home side made 226-7. With eight overs remaining, Sussex were nowhere to be seen on 130-8 but then Goodwin cut loose. Partnered by Pakistan's Mohammad Sami, who made 32 not out, the former Zimbabwean Test batsman scored 87 not out from 64 balls to ensure the trophy would head to Hove.

WEDNESDAY 15th SEPTEMBER 1971

Nathan John Astle was born in Christchurch, New Zealand, and is another overseas international who spent a brief period of his playing career at Trent Bridge. In 1997 he made ten first-class appearances for Nottinghamshire, scoring 644 runs, at an average of 40.25. He made two centuries, both of which were exactly 100, plus three 50s. Astle also grabbed a more-than-useful 22 wickets at 23.86, less than his overall career average of over 32 per wicket. With his right-arm medium-paced bowling, Astle's best return for the county came at Bristol against Gloucestershire when he collected 5-46. He also played nine List A matches, producing 275 runs and 13 more wickets.

THURSDAY 15th SEPTEMBER 2005

Batting against Kent at Canterbury, Nottinghamshire's Jason Gallian was run out for 199. Having already fallen for the same score, also to a run out, against Sussex at Trent Bridge earlier in the same season, Gallian became the first batsman in the history of the game to be dismissed whilst one run short of a double-hundred on two occasions.

THURSDAY 16th SEPTEMBER 2004

Needing just one point to secure the division two Frizzell County Championship title, Nottinghamshire were able to celebrate on the first day of their match with Essex at Trent Bridge as Paul Franks trapped Ronnie Irani lbw to claim a bowling point. Three days later Franks hit the winning run as Notts rounded off their campaign with a three-wicket success.

THURSDAY 16th SEPTEMBER 2010

Beginning the day as third favourites to lift the LV= County Championship title, Nottinghamshire picked up the five bonus points they needed against Lancashire at Old Trafford to leapfrog Somerset and Yorkshire to take the crown. With most of the first three days having been lost to rain the side made it to 400-9 declared – and maximum points – thanks to 126 from Adams Voges and 94 from Samit Patel. Only 4.4 overs were then needed for Ryan Sidebottom (1-6) and Andre Adams (2-3) to take the three wickets needed to start the celebrations.

SATURDAY 17th SEPTEMBER 1988

This was the final day of a championship fixture against Yorkshire at Trent Bridge. Nottinghamshire's West Indian all-rounder Franklyn Stephenson produced a feat that had only happened twice before in first-class cricket, back in 1905 and 1906. He scored a hundred in both innings and also took ten wickets in the same match, enabling him to complete an astonishing double for the season. Having already taken 100 first-class wickets, the big Barbadian needed 210 more runs to also achieve 1,000 for the campaign. Scoring 111 in the first innings, he then hit 117 in the second. If anything was going to put a dampener on the celebrations, it was Yorkshire actually winning the game – by 127 runs!

SUNDAY 17th SEPTEMBER 1989

The domestic Sunday competition in 1989 was sponsored by Refuge Assurance and at the conclusion, the top four sides contested the Refuge Assurance Cup. Nottinghamshire, who finished fourth in the league, defeated Lancashire in the semi-final, with Essex overcoming Worcestershire. The final was played at Edgbaston and having restricted Essex to 160, Tim Robinson's Notts were favoured to lift the silverware but fell five runs short after Derek Pringle claimed figures of 4-20.

SATURDAY 17th SEPTEMBER 2005

Despite still having one match left to play, Nottinghamshire clinched the Frizzell County Championship title when they defeated Kent at Canterbury by 214 runs. Chasing a mammoth 420, the home side were skittled out for 205, with AJ Harris claiming 6-76 to kick-start the celebrations.

SUNDAY 17th SEPTEMBER 2006

Gareth Clough's best bowling performance for Nottinghamshire came during a NatWest Pro40 contest against Sussex at Trent Bridge. The medium-pacer returned 6-25 from his eight overs as the south coast side tumbled to 110 all out and a crushing eight-wicket defeat.

SUNDAY 18th SEPTEMBER 1988

Nottingham-born Luke Jack Fletcher made his Nottinghamshire debut in 2008 and appeared in one Youth Test and three Youth ODIs for England in the same year. The 6'6" tall, medium-fast bowler showed early prowess with the bat with 92 against Hampshire in his fourth championship match. He made five appearances in the 2010 championship-winning campaign before establishing himself as a first-team regular the following year, claiming his first five-wicket haul in a season which brought 48 first-class wickets, including eight in the champion county v MCC match in Abu Dhabi.

SUNDAY 18th SEPTEMBER 1994

Playing against Middlesex at Trent Bridge, in the AXA Equity and Law League, Nottinghamshire's Greg Mike became only the second batsman in English domestic List A cricket (after Surrey's DM Smith in 1982) to be given out handled the ball. He hadn't even scored a run when the incident happened!

WEDNESDAY 19th SEPTEMBER 2007

At Kingsmead, Durban, in the World Twenty20, India's Yuvraj Singh became the first cricketer to score six sixes in an over in an international fixture between two Test nations. The unfortunate bowler on the receiving end was England's Stuart Broad, who had just left Leicestershire having agreed to move to Trent Bridge for the 2008 season.

TUESDAY 20th SEPTEMBER 2011

For the second time in a few weeks Andre Adams was left cursing his luck against Somerset. Having been a member of the Nottinghamshire side that lost to them in the quarter-finals of the English domestic Twenty20, he then had to endure more bitter disappointment with Auckland Aces. The Kiwis' involvement in the Champions League ended when they were defeated by the south-west county in the qualifying tournament in Hyderabad.

THURSDAY 21st SEPTEMBER 2006

There were many contrasting emotions at Trent Bridge as Darren Bicknell bowed out of first-class cricket. The left-handed opener scored 19,931 runs during his 20 years in the game, the last seven years with Nottinghamshire. Being dismissed twice in the day, as his side slumped to relegation, wasn't an ideal way for him to step down and he then had to watch as Sussex completed the win that secured the first division title. The defeat meant that Notts were condemned to life in the second tier after winning the championship themselves just 12 months earlier.

SUNDAY 22nd SEPTEMBER 1861

Francis Joseph "Frank" Shacklock was a quick right-arm bowler, who picked up 360 wickets for Nottinghamshire. His best performance with the ball was 8-32, against MCC at Lord's in 1887. Shacklock was good friends with county team-mate Mordecai Sherwin and the pair would often turn out together for MCC. It's said that the name of Arthur Conan Doyle's most famous character, Sherlock Holmes, came from an amalgamation of the pair's surnames after Doyle spent a day watching them perform. Shacklock, who was born in Crich, Derbyshire, later moved to New Zealand, where he died in 1937.

FRIDAY 23rd SEPTEMBER 2011

Deputising for injured Nottinghamshire team-mate Stuart Broad, Graeme Swann captained England for the first time in a Twenty20 international against the West Indies at The Oval. A magnificent team performance, featuring an unbeaten 62 from another county colleague, Alex Hales, made it a winning start for the new skipper, although two days later the visitors squared the series with a 25-run win on the same ground.

TUESDAY 24th SEPTEMBER 1968

Born in Nottingham, Paul Raymond Pollard represented his home county between 1987 and 1998. A left-handed opening batsman, he made 157 first-class appearances for Notts, scoring 8,347 runs at 32.73. He scored 13 centuries with a best of 180. In 149 List A matches for Nottinghamshire, Pollard added 4,122 runs at an average of 33.24. After leaving Trent Bridge, Pollard spent three seasons playing for Worcestershire.

SUNDAY 25th SEPTEMBER 1881

Henry Clinton Attenburrow died in Jersey, aged 74. He is regarded as the only man to take ten wickets on debut for Nottinghamshire, although no full analyses were ever recorded for either innings. Press reports at the time named him incorrectly as 'K Brown', perhaps because he was on the staff at Nottingham General Hospital as a surgeon. He only played twice for the county before retiring to Jersey in the early 1850s.

SATURDAY 26th SEPTEMBER 1970

Graeme Francis Archer was born in Carlisle and spent eight seasons at Nottinghamshire, scoring 5,354 runs in the 100 first-class matches he played. He scored ten first-class centuries, with a best of 168, plus another two in List A competition.

MONDAY 27th SEPTEMBER 1982

Playing for an International XI against a West Indies XI in Sabina Park, Kingston, Nottinghamshire's Eddie Hemmings took all ten wickets in the home side's first innings. Of all the bowlers who have ever taken ten wickets in an innings of first-class cricket, the off-spinner's analysis of 10-175 contains the most amount of runs conceded.

SUNDAY 27th SEPTEMBER 2009

The final one-day match of Mark Ealham's career coincided with Nottinghamshire making their lowest ever score in List A cricket. Against Gloucestershire at Trent Bridge in the NatWest Pro40 League, the home side were dismissed for just 57 in 18.5 overs. Ealham was one of six batsmen who failed to get off the mark but was then denied the opportunity of adding to his 99 one-day wickets for Notts, as Gloucestershire raced to their nine-wicket win in just 7.3 overs.

SUNDAY 28th SEPTEMBER 1884

The passing of Frederick Morley is one of cricket's sadder tales. The former Nottinghamshire left-arm fast bowler sustained injuries when en route to tour Australia in late 1882. The team's ship was involved in a collision in Colombo on the outbound journey and Morley sustained damage to his ribs, from which he was unable to recover. Alienated from his family, due to his deteriorating health and inability to bring in income, Morley lived in seclusion for the rest of his life and died of congestion and dropsy, aged 33. He was interred with a cricket ball in his favoured left hand.

SUNDAY 29th SEPTEMBER 1957

Brian Christopher "Chris" Broad joined Nottinghamshire in 1984 after making 118 first-class appearances for Gloucestershire. His move to the East Midlands was mutually beneficial as he helped Notts to the 1987 double of county championship and NatWest titles, as well as picking up Benson and Hedges Cup and Sunday League winner's medals. He scored 12,386 runs for Notts in the longer form of the game, plus 6,390 in one-day competition, as well as playing 34 Tests. Son Stuart maintained the family link with the county by moving to Notts from Leicestershire ahead of the 2008 season.

MONDAY 30th SEPTEMBER 1963

Sheffield-born Callum "David" Fraser-Darling was a medium-fast right-arm bowler who made 11 first-class appearances for Nottinghamshire between 1984 and 1988. Amongst his 17 wickets was a best haul of 5-84. Fraser-Darling also played 16 List A matches before leaving to join Nottinghamshire Police at the end of the 1988 season.

NOTTINGHAMSHIRE CCC
On This Day

OCTOBER

MONDAY 1st OCTOBER 2007

Graeme Swann's second one-day international was his first as a Nottinghamshire player. Having appeared for England in South Africa more than seven years earlier, whilst a Northamptonshire player, he had to wait for his next opportunity and it came in Dambulla, Sri Lanka. Swann took 1-47 from ten overs and scored 24 with the bat but the match was convincingly won by the home nation.

FRIDAY 1st OCTOBER 1965

The younger of the two brothers that represented the county, Russell John Evans was born in Calverton and made his Nottinghamshire debut against the Pakistan tourists in 1987. Like brother Kevin, he was a right-handed batsman, and made scores of 4 and 0 on his first appearance and then had to wait a year for another opportunity. In all, he only played for Notts on six occasions in first-class cricket, with just one of those matches coming in the championship. He also played in six List A matches whilst at Trent Bridge but was released at the end of the 1990 season. In 2011 Russell Evans joined the list of first-class umpires.

TUESDAY 2nd OCTOBER 1934

Born in Bedford, Geoff Millman had played Minor Counties cricket for Bedfordshire before being given an opportunity with Nottinghamshire in 1957. Over nine seasons the wicketkeeper claimed 599 dismissals (517 catches and 82 stumpings), with a best of 85 in 1961. A good enough batsman to score over a thousand runs in a season twice in his career, as well as register three centuries, he played six times for England in 1961 and 1962. In later life he ran the family jewellery business back in Bedford, where he died in 2005, at the age of 70.

FRIDAY 3rd OCTOBER 1913

In just nine first-class matches for Nottinghamshire, James Bradley picked up 19 wickets with his slow left-arm bowling. He made his debut against Surrey at The Oval in 1937 and took 4-116 at Canterbury against Kent a week later. These would be the best figures of a career cut short due to the outbreak of war. Born in Pleasley Hill, he died in Mansfield in 2001, at the age of 87.

GRAEME SWANN, THE NUMBER ONE-RANKED BOWLER IN ODI CRICKET 2011

SUNDAY 4th OCTOBER 1925

Alan Keith Walker was born in Manly, New South Wales, and achieved notoriety as a rugby union international before making his mark as a Nottinghamshire joint record-holder. As a centre for Australia, he won five caps and travelled to Britain and France on the 1947/48 tour, scoring 19 tries. He also made two appearances against the Lions in 1950 before allowing his left-arm fast-medium bowling to take precedent. Walker took 97 wickets in 26 matches for his state, and toured South Africa but couldn't force his way into the Test side. Walker then joined Notts between 1954 and 1958, with his most notable performance coming against Leicestershire in 1956 when he took four wickets in four balls, only the second player to achieve the feat for the county. The Australian returned home after retiring from the game and died in Sydney in June 2005, at the age of 79.

MONDAY 4th OCTOBER 1937

Ian Joseph Davison took 540 first-class wickets for Nottinghamshire. Between 1959 and 1966, the Hemel Hempstead-born medium-fast bowler was a virtual ever-present, making 177 appearances for the county. His best figures of 7-28 came against Derbyshire at Trent Bridge in 1962. That was just one of 22 separate occasions in which he took five or more wickets in an innings and twice he claimed ten in a match. Davison's career encompassed the early days of limited-overs cricket and he featured in five Gillette Cup ties for Notts, plus three more for Bedfordshire, where he played after leaving the first-class game.

THURSDAY 4th OCTOBER 1979

Adam Charles Voges cemented his place in Nottinghamshire folklore with an innings of 126 that helped secure the county championship title on the final day of the 2010 season. He first played for Notts in 2008, at the start of a relationship with the county that often saw him sharing the overseas role with fellow Australian David Hussey. Fifteen ODI and four Twenty20 international appearances for his country, between 2007 and 2011, confirmed Voges' talent as a high-quality, right-handed top-order batsman. Born in Subiaco, near Perth, he skippered Notts for the first time during the latter stages of the 2011 Friends Provident Twenty20 campaign.

WEDNESDAY 5th OCTOBER 1960

Left-handed batsman Neil Weightman only made four first-class appearances for Nottinghamshire, a little disappointing considering he scored a century in the second, 105 against Leicestershire at Hinckley in 1981. Born at Normanton-on-Trent, Weightman made eight List A appearances for Notts, which produced only 44 runs.

TUESDAY 6th OCTOBER 1936

Robert Arthur "Bob" White was born in Fulham and began his career with Middlesex in 1958. Although he later developed into a true all-rounder, he was selected purely as a batsman at Lord's. After moving to Nottinghamshire in 1966 he developed his off-spin to such an extent that he took 693 first-class wickets after the age of 29, with a best of 7-41 coming against Derbyshire at Ilkeston. White's batting still continued to serve Notts well and he scored 8,259 runs for them in his 298 matches, with a best score of 116 not out against Surrey at The Oval.

WEDNESDAY 6th OCTOBER 1982

Muhammad "Nadeem" Malik was born in Nottingham and played for his home county before going on to experience regular first-team cricket with Worcestershire and Leicestershire. Malik gained first-team experience with Nottinghamshire in 2001, claiming Worcestershire's Graeme Hick as his maiden first-class wicket. In 15 matches, the right-arm medium-pacer took 37 wickets at 36.29 each. Just ten more came in 20 List A matches though, a strike-rate he significantly improved upon after moving to New Road in 2004.

SUNDAY 7th OCTOBER 2007

Nottinghamshire's trio of England bowlers almost collected a clean sweep of the Sri Lankan wickets in an ODI in Dambulla and then came up with vital runs to secure a two-wicket victory. Batting first, the home side were dismissed for 162, with Graeme Swann taking 4-34, Ryan Sidebottom 3-19 and Stuart Broad picking up 2-26. The other wicket to fall was a run out, inflicted by Swann, who then confirmed the man of the match award by scoring a quick-fire 25 before leaving it to his county colleagues to see England home. Broad ended on 20 not out and Sidebottom was unbeaten on seven.

TUESDAY 8th OCTOBER 1946

Robert Bagguley died at his home at Brackcliffe Farm, Bradmore, Nottinghamshire, aged 73. An all-rounder, who batted right-handed but bowled left-arm slow-medium, he played 48 games for his home county between 1891 and 1896 and was only 17 when making an impact on debut, taking 6-74 against Sussex at Hove. The same opposition were the recipients of his only first-class century, five years later. The 5'3" tall batsman scored 110 against them at Trent Bridge, with 102 coming on the second morning alone.

THURSDAY 9th OCTOBER 1834

In order to bring their own young players through into the county side, Nottinghamshire allowed local clubs to nominate 22 youngsters to face a Notts XI in a two-day practice match in 1861. Although seven of the 22 went on to play first-class cricket, Walter Price had to wait until he was in his mid-30s before making his only five appearances. He did, however, make 20 appearances for MCC as a right-handed batsman. Price had four cricket-playing sons, one of whom, Alfred, made three appearances for Notts in 1897. Born in Ruddington, he also died there in 1894.

FRIDAY 10th OCTOBER 1856

George Savile Foljambe was educated at Eton and then Christ Church, Oxford, before going on to make seven appearances for Nottinghamshire. Born at Osberton Hall, he later became a JP and Deputy Lieutenant for Nottinghamshire, as well as Lieutenant-Colonel of the 4th Volunteer Battalion of the Sherwood Foresters. His father, FJS Foljambe, became president of the Nottinghamshire club in 1887 and his brother-in-law, William Bury, also played for the county. Foljambe died in London in 1920.

WEDNESDAY 10th OCTOBER 2007

After picking up three wickets three days earlier, Ryan Sidebottom was again at the forefront of the England bowling as they defeated Sri Lanka in an ODI in Colombo. The Nottinghamshire left-arm quickie returned figures of 10-2-37-3 in his side's victory, which also ensured a win in the five-match series. Sidebottom's 12 wickets had come at a cost of just 13.83 runs each and earned him the man of the series award.

MONDAY 11th OCTOBER 2004

Keith Ross Miller MBE was 84 when he died in Mornington, Victoria. Although his impact on Nottinghamshire was slight, one appearance right at the very end of his career, he did garnish it with a brilliant century against Cambridge University at Trent Bridge. In 55 Tests for Australia he had scored 2,958 runs and taken 170 wickets.

THURSDAY 12th OCTOBER 2000

Mark Saxelby was said to be suffering from depression when he committed suicide by ingesting weedkiller. Younger brother of former county seamer Kevin Saxelby, the left-handed batsman had made his Nottinghamshire debut in 1989, scoring 4 and 32 not out against Cambridge University. In 58 first-class innings he failed to get past 77, although he did reach three figures in the AXA Equity and Law League at Chester-le-Street in 1993. Following that performance he moved to Durham and began life with his new county by scoring 181 on his championship debut for them, at Chesterfield against Derbyshire. After spells in Minor Counties cricket with Cheshire and Cornwall, he returned to the first-class game with a one-off appearance for Derbyshire three months before his death.

TUESDAY 12th OCTOBER 2010

Four weeks after helping Nottinghamshire lift the county championship, Darren Pattinson began the Australian domestic season still on a high. Playing for his state side, Victoria, the quick bowler took a career-best 8-35 at the start of a four-day match against Western Australia in Perth. One of his victims was Trent Bridge team-mate Adam Voges, whom he dismissed lbw for 0.

THURSDAY 13th OCTOBER 1887

George McKenzie Kettle died at Dallicotte House, a large residence outside Bridgnorth in Shropshire, and on his death certificate his occupation was simply described as a "gentleman". He was born in Leicestershire in 1810 and played most of his club cricket at Burton-on-Trent. Of his 15 first-class outings, the majority were for MCC, with just one of them for Nottinghamshire. Against Hampshire at Trent Bridge in 1843, he scored just three runs and didn't bowl a single ball as Notts won by an innings.

FRIDAY 14th OCTOBER 1983

Treliske, Cornwall, was the birthplace of Neil James Edwards, a left-handed opening batsman who had scored three centuries in his 49 first-class appearances for Somerset. Joining Nottinghamshire ahead of the 2010 season, he played six championship matches, making a top score of 85 against Kent but his campaign was restricted by a broken hand. A further injury setback, a broken arm sustained whilst batting at Hove, disrupted his 2011 season, although he returned to score 49 in the Second XI Trophy Final against Lancashire.

FRIDAY 15th OCTOBER 1915

Ralph Eustace Hemingway was killed in action as a Second Lieutenant with the Sherwood Foresters in France. The former right-handed batsman had made 30 first-class appearances for Nottinghamshire between 1903 and 1905, scoring a total of 944 runs. He was 37 when he lost his life at Hohenzollen, near Vermelles.

THURSDAY 16th OCTOBER 1834

Left-arm fast bowler George Wootton was born in Clifton, Nottinghamshire. Handy enough with a bat to have registered five 50s, his real prowess was with the ball. Between 1861 and 1871 he took 180 wickets in 52 matches for Notts. Aside from his playing commitments with the county, Wootton was a regular performer for the All England Eleven that toured the country and took a career-best 10-54 against Yorkshire at Bramall Lane. In all first-class matches he took a staggering 983 wickets at an average of just 13.

WEDNESDAY 16th OCTOBER 1872

Born in Sutton-in-Ashfield in 1806, Thomas Heath was the first player from that town to represent the Nottingham club. He was an outstanding all-rounder, renowned for his catching, fielding and throwing. In 20 county matches Heath didn't score more than 35 but he was very popular and considered to be a bit of a wag, despite profound deafness. In 1839 he emigrated to France and grew so stout that his friends couldn't recognise him when he returned five years later. Heath met with a sad end to life. After visiting his brother in Sutton, he had a fit and lay unconscious for a week before dying.

MONDAY 16th OCTOBER 1944

The answer to the question "who was at the other end?" is John Parkin. Born at Kimberley, Nottinghamshire, the right-handed batsman had a modest first-class career but had the best seat in the house for one of cricket's champagne moments. Against Glamorgan at Swansea in 1968, Parkin was the non-striker as Garfield Sobers launched Malcolm Nash into the stratosphere on six consecutive occasions. Whilst the direct combatants had their own stories to tell, Parkin's own memory of the occasion must be tinged with sadness as it was his final championship appearance for his home county. Making 15 not out and 9 not out still only nudged his average above 11 but because of a brilliant West Indian his place in the history books is assured – even if it's only as a quiz question!

THURSDAY 17th OCTOBER 1996

Paul Strang spent one season at Trent Bridge. Eighteen months before his debut for Nottinghamshire he scored his only Test century. The Zimbabwean leg-break and googly bowler showed his worth with the bat by scoring 106 not out against Pakistan at the Sheikhupura Stadium in Sialkot. Strang then put in a decent shift with the ball, bowling 69 overs and taking 5-212 during the Pakistan first innings, in which Wasim Akram made an unbeaten 257.

WEDNESDAY 18th OCTOBER 1989

Few cricketers can have made less of an impact than John Reddish did on his only first-class outing. Having been a second XI regular for three seasons, the leg-break and googly bowler got his opportunity against Oxford University at Trent Bridge in 1930. Last man in, he made 2 not out in the Nottinghamshire innings. When the students batted, Reddish wheeled away for 27 overs without success, ending with figures of 0-125. Reddish was 84 when he died in Manchester.

TUESDAY 19th OCTOBER 2010

Having been guests of honour at a Lord's Taverners luncheon, Nottinghamshire's players and staff then visited Buckingham Palace, where they were presented with the LV= County Championship trophy and medals by HRH The Duke of Edinburgh.

WEDNESDAY 20th OCTOBER 1976

Having spent a decade at Warwickshire, right-handed batsman Mark Anant Wagh joined Nottinghamshire ahead of the 2007 season. He was player of the year in his first season, the start of a five-year stint which brought 4,378 runs at an average of 40.91. Born in Birmingham, he left cricket midway through the 2011 season, aged 34, to pursue a career in law.

THURSDAY 20th OCTOBER 2011

Playing against India in an ODI in Mohali, Samit Patel scored a quick-fire 70 from just 43 deliveries for England. His performance won the Nottinghamshire all-rounder a sponsor's prize of a brand new motorcycle. After abortive attempts to get it flown back to the UK, Patel agreed to let an equivalent cash sum be paid into the players' tour fund instead!

SATURDAY 21st OCTOBER 1882

Sir Julien Cahn was an entrepreneur and philanthropist, who became a great benefactor of Nottinghamshire cricket. Born in Cardiff, he inherited a fortune from his father and turned his attention to the pursuit of his favourite game. Twice president of the county club, his donations helped pay for two stands, a new scoreboard and an indoor training facility at Trent Bridge. He also built a new ground at West Park in West Bridgford and set up his own team, the Sir Julien Cahn XI, which would feature many stars of the day.

FRIDAY 22nd OCTOBER 1948

Lively, fast-medium seam bowler Mike Hendrick was, undoubtedly, one of the best of his generation. Born in Darley Dale, Derbyshire, the bulk of his career was spent with his home county, for whom he took 497 wickets in 167 matches. He played 30 Tests for England, plus 22 ODIs, including the 1979 Prudential World Cup Final against the West Indies at Lord's. He moved to Trent Bridge in 1982, taking exactly 100 wickets in 34 first-class outings for his new county. Hendrick was briefly a first-class umpire before turning his attention to coaching. He managed the Nottinghamshire first-team in 1992 and later used his experience to develop and coach the county's young seamers.

MIKE SMEDLEY, NOTTINGHAMSHIRE CAPTAIN AND LATER CLUB PRESIDENT

WEDNESDAY 23rd OCTOBER 1878

Alfred Clarke was the son of William Clarke, who developed Trent Bridge and set up the All England Eleven. Born at the Bell Inn, where his father was the landlord, it was understandable that he inherited a love of the game, although his ability may be brought into question. He was regarded as a "regular long-leg fieldsman" and his longevity in the side would appear to have more in common with nepotism than ability. Clarke made one decent contribution, a score of 57, in his 24 matches for the county before setting himself up as a maltster and publican in Ruddington, where he died on this day, aged 47.

SUNDAY 24th OCTOBER 1999

Nottinghamshire has enjoyed a fine relationship with New Zealand cricketers over the years. Four of the Kiwis who spent some time at Trent Bridge all appeared for their national team together in a Test against India in Kanpur. Daniel Vettori took 6-67 in the home side's first innings, Chris Cairns scored 55 runs in the match, Stephen Fleming 33 and Nathan Astle hit 39 and took 2-27.

MONDAY 25th OCTOBER 1830

Born in Southwell, Robert Crispin "Cris"Tinley followed his two elder brothers, Francis (19 matches) and Vincent (just one match), in playing for Nottinghamshire. Cris was by far the most talented, particularly with the ball, although his action was described as "underarm right-arm slow". In 54 matches he took 138 wickets at 14.99, with a best of 8-12.

THURSDAY 25th OCTOBER 1979

The tallest player to ever represent Nottinghamshire was born in Derby but played his first county cricket for Essex before moving to Trent Bridge. At 6'10", in terms of height, William Ingleby Jefferson has had few equals in the history of the game. He joined Notts in time for the 2007 season, having made a couple of appearances for England A in Bangladesh during the previous winter. During his time at Nottingham, the right-handed batsman played 22 first-class matches, making one century, plus 24 List A and 23 Twenty20 games.

SUNDAY 26th OCTOBER 1969

David Barrington Pennett was born in Leeds and spent a couple of years in Yorkshire's second team before moving to Trent Bridge. His out-of-season profession as a male model earned as many headlines as his abilities on the field but his wholehearted commitment brought 60 wickets in 31 matches, with a best of 5-36. Pennett's right-arm fast-medium bowling brought 44 wickets in one-day competition.

FRIDAY 27th OCTOBER 1865

Better known for his prowess as a footballer with Nottingham Forest and England, Dr Tinsley Lindley also made four first-class appearances for Nottinghamshire in 1888. He had earlier played at Cambridge University as a right-handed batsman of limited ability and as a slow right-arm bowler. Born in Nottingham, he only scored 64 runs for his home county and took just one wicket, figures that pale alongside his tally of 14 goals from 13 England football internationals. On retirement, he turned his attention to his law practice, becoming a lecturer at the University of Nottingham, as well as a County Court Judge. Awarded the OBE in 1918, he died in the city of his birth in 1940, aged 74.

TUESDAY 28th OCTOBER 1941

A magnificent servant to Nottinghamshire cricket, Michael John Smedley was born at Maltby, Yorkshire, and played for that county's second string until getting his chance at Trent Bridge. A stylish right-handed batsman, he made his Notts first-class debut against Northamptonshire in 1964. His breakthrough innings came in the following season when he made 107 against Derbyshire, the first of 28 centuries Smedley would score for the county. In all, he played 357 matches, scoring 16,414 runs at 31.26 each. Captain of the club between 1975 and 1979, he also scored a further 3,674 runs in limited-overs matches.

THURSDAY 28th OCTOBER 1971

Australian Test batsman Greg Blewett played 16 first-class matches for Nottinghamshire during the 2001 season. Born on this day in North Adelaide, South Australia, he scored 1,292 runs for the county, at an average of 47.85. The largest of his five tons was 137 not out against Durham at Chester-le-Street.

SATURDAY 29th OCTOBER 2011

Any time the Australians are beaten at cricket it's a case of celebration for an English cricketer, even if it was in the Hong Kong International Cricket Sixes in Kowloon. Nottinghamshire's Chris Read made 32 from just eight deliveries faced, with four sixes and two fours, as his side reached their target of 87-4 in only 4.2 overs. The following day, in the final, England were 'Razzaq-ed' as Pakistan made a colossal score of 154-5 in just five overs, with Abdul Razzaq blasting 63 from 17 balls.

SATURDAY 30th OCTOBER 1971

Having amassed eight years of first-class experience in South Africa, Gregory James "Greg" Smith was seen as an astute signing when manager Clive Rice persuaded him to sign for Nottinghamshire in 2001. Born in Pretoria but able to play as a dual-national thanks to his English father, Smith was a revelation at Trent Bridge with his aggressive left-arm new-ball bowling and hard-hitting lower-order batting. In 77 matches he picked up 251 dismissals at an average of 26.69. On 11 occasions he took five wickets or more in an innings, with a best analysis of 8-53 coming against Essex at Trent Bridge in 2002. In his penultimate season with the club, 2005, he took 51 wickets as Nottinghamshire lifted the county championship. In Smith's five years of county cricket he also took a further 116 wickets in 85 List A games.

MONDAY 31st OCTOBER 2011

West Indies batsman Darren Bravo scored his maiden Test century, playing against Bangladesh in Mirpur. The left-hander, who had completed a stint with Nottinghamshire just a month earlier, went on to score 195 in the 229-run victory. His runs came from 297 balls, with 12 fours and five sixes.

NOTTINGHAMSHIRE CCC
On This Day

NOVEMBER

SATURDAY 1st NOVEMBER 1884

Sheffield-born Lionel Kirk only played 14 first-class matches for Nottinghamshire, yet found himself skippering the side at the nervy conclusion of the 1927 season. With Arthur Carr ill, Kirk led the side at Swansea, knowing a win over Glamorgan would secure the championship. Blowing their lines spectacularly, they fell to an innings defeat, a result that meant the title went to Lancashire instead.

THURSDAY 1st NOVEMBER 1923

Bruce Dooland was born at Cowandilla, near Adelaide. The leg-break and googly bowler had played three Tests for Australia before joining Nottinghamshire in 1953. It was the start of an association which would last for five years and span 140 matches, during which he took 770 wickets at 18.86, and scored 4,782 runs at an average of 24.52. His haul of 181 victims in 1954 has never been bettered for the county.

SATURDAY 1st NOVEMBER 2008

Three Nottinghamshire players missed out on a substantial pay-day when they appeared for England against the Stanford Super Stars at Coolidge in Antigua. The brainchild of the Texan financier Allen Stanford, the tournament ended with a winner-takes-all match, with the two sides playing a Twenty20 game of cricket for $20 million (around £12.25m). Sadly for the England side there was to be no rich harvest as they were humbled for just 99, with Samit Patel top-scoring with 22, Stuart Broad making 9 not out and Graeme Swann 3. The home team, made up of West Indian players, knocked off the runs quickly to win by ten wickets.

MONDAY 2nd NOVEMBER 1835

Richard Daft was born in Nottingham on this day and went on to become a regular member of the All England Eleven, before making his first appearance for his home county in 1858. He eventually played in 157 first-class matches for Nottinghamshire, captaining them from 1871 until 1880. He then became a partner in the Radcliffe-on-Trent Brewery and later the proprietor of the Trent Bridge Inn. Daft's father-in-law Butler Parr, brother Charles Daft and two sons Harry Daft and Richard P Daft also played for Nottinghamshire.

FRIDAY 3rd NOVEMBER 1944

Reg Simpson played 495 first-class matches during his career but the very first came whilst stationed in India during the war. Invited to play for Sind against Bombay in the Ranji Trophy, he made scores of 88 and 63 in the drawn contest.

MONDAY 4th NOVEMBER 1901

John "Foghorn" Jackson died in extreme poverty at Brownlow Hill, a workhouse in Liverpool. During his playing career he had been regarded as the quickest and most fearsome bowler of his generation. For Nottinghamshire, Foghorn made 33 appearances between 1855 and 1866, taking 140 wickets at 14.31, with a best of 9-49 against Surrey at The Oval in 1860. Jackson was 68 at the time of his death.

THURSDAY 5th NOVEMBER 1987

Two Nottinghamshire players helped England overcome the challenge of India in the World Cup semi-final at the Wankhede Stadium in Bombay. Batsman Tim Robinson scored 13 out of his side's total of 254-6 before off-spinner Eddie Hemmings, collecting the best bowling figures of his 33-match ODI career, returned 4-52 as India were dismissed for 219.

WEDNESDAY 6th NOVEMBER 1918

Born in Carcroft in Yorkshire, Frederick Wilfred "Freddie" Stocks was 27 before he forced his way into Nottinghamshire's championship side. Once there, though, he proved difficult to dislodge, with his final match coming in July 1957, by which time he was 38. In 243 matches for the county, the left-handed batsman scored 11,397 runs at an average of 29.60. On five occasions he passed a thousand runs, 1951 being his best year when he amassed 1,396 at 34.04. Stocks scored 13 centuries for the county, with a best of 171 coming against the touring Australians in 1956.

THURSDAY 7th NOVEMBER 1940

John Cotton took exactly 400 wickets for Nottinghamshire between 1958 and 1964, with a best of 7-73 against Somerset at Trent Bridge in 1959. Born in Newstead, Nottinghamshire, the right-arm fast-medium bowler played 138 matches, taking his wickets at 25.92 each.

SUNDAY 8th NOVEMBER 1987

The World Cup final at Eden Gardens, Calcutta, went the way of Australia, who defeated England by seven runs. There was disappointment for Nottinghamshire's Tim Robinson, dismissed without scoring, whilst county team-mate Eddie Hemmings was England's most successful bowler with 2-48.

SATURDAY 9th NOVEMBER 1985

The finest of many fine cricketing days for Richard Hadlee came at the Gabba in Brisbane. Spearheading the New Zealand attack in the opening Test against Australia, the Nottinghamshire all-rounder took a career-best 9-52. Of the dismissed batsmen, only Geoff Lawson escaped his clutches but even he was caught by Hadlee (from the bowling of Vaughan Brown). A score of 54 with the bat – and then second-innings figures of 6-71 (giving overall match figures of 15-123) made the decision of the man of the match selector something of a formality!

SUNDAY 10th NOVEMBER 1991

South Africa's lengthy exile from international cricket denied Clive Rice the opportunity of playing at the highest level until late in his career. The former Nottinghamshire all-rounder was 42 by the time he made the first of just three one-day international appearances. Captaining his country, against India in Calcutta, Rice scored 14 and failed to take a wicket in a three-wicket defeat.

TUESDAY 11th NOVEMBER 1930

Former England Test batsman William "Dodger" Whysall died in Nottingham, aged 43. He made 346 appearances for Nottinghamshire, scoring 20,376 runs at an average of just under 40. His runs included exactly 50 centuries, which included three double-hundreds and a best of 248. As a consistent right-handed batsman, he went on the 1924-25 tour of Australia and played three Tests, scoring 75 at Adelaide and 76 at Melbourne. Whysall's best season brought 2,716 runs at 51.24 as Notts stormed to the 1929 county championship. A recall to the England side for his fourth and final Test only brought scores of 13 and 10, as he bowed out of cricket in 1930. Two months later he slipped on a dance floor and injured his elbow, dying two weeks later of septicaemia.

TIM ROBINSON, SECOND ON THE NOTTS ALL-TIME RUN-SCORERS' LIST

THURSDAY 12th NOVEMBER 1942

Michael Norman Somerset Taylor was born in Amersham, Buckinghamshire, and played for Nottinghamshire and Hampshire during a first-class career from 1964 to 1980. A right-arm medium-pace bowler, his best season for Notts was 1968 when he took 99 wickets at just 21 each. He made 230 first-class appearances and 80 List A outings whilst at Trent Bridge, claiming 522 wickets in the former and 107 in the shorter format. Despite his 'third' name it was Mike's twin brother, Derek, who spent his first-class career playing for Somerset!

WEDNESDAY 13th NOVEMBER 1839

Born in St Ann's, Nottingham, Michael McIntyre was the eldest of three brothers who played first-class cricket for Nottinghamshire. Martin made 45 appearances and William 14. Michael, although considered to be just as talented, only played in one county match, against Kent in 1864. He did make two appearances for the North of England against Surrey and also played for Notts at Trent Bridge against the Free Foresters, taking 9-18, but the opposition fielded 14 players so the match didn't attain first-class status. McIntyre was then engaged as a professional by Thomas Walker at the new ground in Eastwood but he later fell on hard times and died at Basford Workhouse of phthisis (also known as consumption) on 9th October 1888.

MONDAY 14th NOVEMBER 1904

Born in Nuncargate, Nottinghamshire, Harold Larwood's career path seemed destined to lead him to a life spent underground, when he left school at 14 to work down the local coal mine. Early performances for the Kirkby Portland club earned him a county trial – and the rest, as they say, is history. Although best known for his role in the Bodyline series of 1932/33, Nottinghamshire followers may instead reflect on the outstanding figures left by one of their greatest talents. The fast bowler played for them in 300 matches between 1924 and 1938, taking 1,247 wickets at an average of 16.24. He passed 100 wickets in a season on eight occasions, 1932 his best when he removed 162 batsmen. Larwood retired to Australia and passed away on 22nd July 1995, aged 90.

TUESDAY 15th NOVEMBER 2011

Riki Wessels scored a career high 197, batting for Mid West Rhinos against Matabeleland Tuskers at Bulawayo, Zimbabwe. The hard-hitting batsman had just come off his first season at Nottinghamshire to return for his third campaign with the Rhinos. Son of the former dual-Test batsman Kepler Wessels – who had played for Australia and South Africa – Riki scored his runs from 286 balls, with 12 fours and nine sixes.

SATURDAY 16th NOVEMBER 1985

Having accepted a short-term contract to play first-class cricket in South Africa, as captain of Orange Free State, Chris Broad appeared seven times for the Bloemfontein-based club. The Nottinghamshire opener scored 416 runs at an average of 37.81, his one century coming against Natal at Kingsmead, Durban, where he made an undefeated 101.

THURSDAY 17th NOVEMBER 1960

Mark Andrew Fell made one century for Nottinghamshire, 108 against Essex at Trent Bridge in 1982. Born in Newark on this day, the right-handed batsman made 15 first-class and 19 List A appearances for the county before briefly playing for Derbyshire, ahead of a lengthy career in Minor Counties cricket with Lincolnshire.

THURSDAY 17th NOVEMBER 2011

Nottinghamshire and England spinner Graeme Swann was announced as the BBC East Midlands Sports Personality of the Year. During the preceding 12 months, the bowler had risen to the top of the world ODI rankings, as well as helping his country retain the Ashes and become the number one-ranked Test side.

SATURDAY 18th NOVEMBER 1876

James Lillywhite's touring XI met a South Australia 22 at the Adelaide Oval and Nottinghamshire's Alf Shaw had a match to remember. The home side were dismissed for 54 in their first innings, the quick bowler returning figures of 56.2-46-12-14. Although an over only constituted four deliveries Shaw's efforts remain impressive, nevertheless, particularly as he then took 7-25 in the second innings – not many bowlers can say they've picked up 21 wickets in the same match!

TUESDAY 19th NOVEMBER 1963

Robert Andrew "Andy" Pick was born in Nottingham and made his debut for the county side in 1983. A lively, fast-medium right-arm bowler, he went on to take 454 wickets at 34.44, with a best of 7-128 coming against Leicestershire at Grace Road in 1990. Pick also played 197 List A matches, picking up a further 233 wickets. A member of the championship-winning squad of 1987, he also played in the losing 1985 Lord's NatWest final against Essex, plus the victory in the same competition against Northamptonshire two years later.

WEDNESDAY 19th NOVEMBER 1986

Steven John Mullaney was born in Warrington, Cheshire, and joined Nottinghamshire ahead of the 2010 season after starting his career with Lancashire. He began life at his new county by scoring an unbeaten century on debut at The Rose Bowl against Hampshire. A member of the side that reached Twenty20 Finals Day in his first season, the right-handed batsman and right-arm medium-pace bowler appeared in 11 matches as Notts clinched the county championship, including the final Old Trafford fixture against his former employers.

WEDNESDAY 20th NOVEMBER 1912

Right-handed batsman and right-arm fast-medium bowler Joseph Herbert Buxton was born in Kirkby-in-Ashfield. A member of the Bentinck Colliery side, he played a handful of second XI matches for the county before making his only championship appearance against Gloucestershire at Trent Bridge in 1937.

MONDAY 21st NOVEMBER 1870

Harvey Staunton was born in the family manor, Staunton Hall, in the Vale of Belvoir. His prowess as a right-handed batsman developed at Bromsgrove School but he had to wait until 1903 before getting an opportunity in first-class cricket. In all, he made 16 appearances for Nottinghamshire, scoring 456 runs, with a top score of 78, made at Trent Bridge against Middlesex. He skippered the second XI in 1909 and 1910 before entering military service during the First World War. Having taken Holy Orders, he served as a chaplain with the Indian Expeditionary Force. Reverend Harvey Staunton was killed in Mesopotamia (modern-day Iraq) on 14th January 1918 and is buried in Baghdad.

CHRIS BROAD WAS ENGLAND'S ASHES HERO IN 1986

FRIDAY 21st NOVEMBER 1958

Robert Timothy "Tim" Robinson ranks second – behind George Gunn – on the list of Nottinghamshire's all-time run scorers. His total of 24,439 came from 374 matches between 1978 and 1999. Born in Sutton-in-Ashfield, the right-handed opener passed 1,000 runs in a season 14 times, with a best of 2,032 in 1984. His top score of 220 not out came against Yorkshire at Trent Bridge. Robinson, who played 29 Tests for England, captained Notts from 1988 to 1995, leading them to the 1989 Benson and Hedges Cup success at Lord's with a man of the match performance.

SATURDAY 22nd NOVEMBER 1997

Proving there was still life in the old dog, 48-year-old Clive Rice skippered the South African Masters to victory over a World Masters XI at Kingsmead, Durban. The former Nottinghamshire all-rounder took 4-35, clean-bowling long-time county colleague Derek Randall for 23.

WEDNESDAY 23rd NOVEMBER 1960

Nigel John Bartle Illingworth made his Nottinghamshire debut in 1981, against Cambridge University at Fenner's. Over the next couple of years, the medium-pace bowler took 16 wickets at an average of 43.37, with a best of 5-89, which came against Middlesex in 1982. Born in Chesterfield, Illingworth made 21 List A appearances for Notts, collecting 23 wickets at 34.65. He left the county at the end of the 1983 season and later played for Lincolnshire in the Minor Counties Championship.

MONDAY 24th NOVEMBER 1873

Reputedly one of Nottinghamshire's quickest round-arm bowlers James "Jemmy" Grundy died of gout at the Midland Hotel, Carrington, where he was the landlord. Born in 1924, he didn't make his debut until the age of 27 but in the next 16 seasons missed only one match. He was the unwilling victim of a piece of cricket history at Lord's in 1857 when he became the first cricketer to be given out handled the ball whilst playing for MCC against Kent. Grundy's best bowling performance for Notts was 9-19 against Kent at Trent Bridge in 1864. His 181 wickets cost only 12.45 runs each.

THURSDAY 24th NOVEMBER 1892

Gifted sportsman Willis Walker was born in Gosforth, but moved to Sheffield where he played league football for a number of sides until cricket took over. He joined Nottinghamshire in 1913 and made seven appearances before the outbreak of war. Returning to Trent Bridge in 1922, Walker went on to score 18,242 runs for the county in 405 matches. He topped 1,000 in a season ten times and reached 31 centuries, with a best of 165 not out. He later set up home in Keighley and died there in 1991, aged 99.

WEDNESDAY 25th NOVEMBER 1936

A hockey and cricket Blue for Oxford University, Andrew John Corran played for Nottinghamshire between 1961 and 1965, skippering them in 1962. Predominantly a medium-pace bowler, he made 101 first-class appearances for the county, taking a healthy 302 wickets at 27.30. Born in Norfolk, his best figures of 6-31 came against Somerset at Bath in his final season, although he had taken a seven-for during his earlier student days. With a top score of 75, he scored 1,829 first-class runs for Notts at 15.63.

FRIDAY 26th NOVEMBER 1886

Nottinghamshire's Wilf Flowers took 1,188 first-class wickets during his career. One performance that can't be included came at the Golbourn Showground, New South Wales. Playing for Alf Shaw's XI, the off-break bowler took 7-35, as the home side were humbled in their first innings for 83. The reason the match was not considered first-class is because the home team, Golbourn, had 18 players – but were still beaten by an innings.

SUNDAY 27th NOVEMBER 1859

Better known for his footballing prowess than for his cricketing career, Henry "Harry" Cursham was born at Wilford. The former Notts County striker holds the record for scoring the most goals in FA Cup football – 49, five ahead of Ian Rush. Cursham won eight caps for his country, scoring five times, including a hat-trick against Ireland. He played just two cricket matches for Nottinghamshire – 24 years apart. He kept wicket against Surrey in 1880 and the touring South Africans in 1904.

WEDNESDAY 28th NOVEMBER 1984

The first of Tim Robinson's 29 Tests for England came at the Wankhede Stadium, Bombay. Opening alongside Lancashire's Graeme Fowler, Robinson made 22 and 1 in an eight-wicket success for India.

SUNDAY 28th NOVEMBER 2004

Having played his final match for Nottinghamshire two months earlier, the Hampshire-bound Kevin Pietersen made his England debut in an ODI against Zimbabwe in Harare. Batting at number five, he scored an unbeaten 27 to guide his side to their victory target for a five-wicket success.

SATURDAY 29th NOVEMBER 1952

William Henry "Dusty" Hare became better known as an expert goal-kicking, rugby union full-back who won 25 caps for England and toured New Zealand with the British Lions in 1983. Born in Newark and then employed on the family farm, he made ten first-class appearances for Nottinghamshire between 1971 and 1977, achieving a top score of 36 with the bat. He also played in seven List A matches before his rugby career began to dominate.

TUESDAY 29th NOVEMBER 1977

Pakistan international Younis Khan played five first-class and three List A matches for Nottinghamshire during the 2005 season. Born in Mardan, Pakistan, his highest score for the county came in a championship fixture at Cardiff, when he made 53 against Glamorgan.

FRIDAY 30th NOVEMBER 1984

Right-handed batsman and slow left-arm spinner Samit Rohit Patel was born in Leicester and made his Nottinghamshire debut in 2002 aged 17. Having represented England at youth level he advanced to full international status, winning his first ODI cap against Scotland at Edinburgh in 2008. Patel took the vital catch which secured the 2010 LV= County Championship title for Notts and the following year, as well as adding to a burgeoning list of ODI appearances, he made his Twenty20 International debut and passed 1,000 runs in a season for the first time. Patel's younger brother, Akhil Patel, made 11 List A and five first-class appearances for Notts between 2007 and 2011.

NOTTINGHAMSHIRE CCC
On This Day

DECEMBER

FRIDAY 1st DECEMBER 1871

George Philip Arthur Stanhope lived a full and varied life. Also known as the 7th Earl of Chesterfield, he served as a soldier and a politician, following his private education at Eton. He became one of the pioneers of Derbyshire cricket, playing for them against the All England Eleven, before playing twice for Nottinghamshire, both against Surrey at Trent Bridge, with a top score of 14. A good friend of the Prince of Wales, he stayed with him at Londesborough Lodge in Scarborough. Both contracted typhoid fever there – the Prince recovered but the Earl's condition deteriorated and he died on this day, aged just 40.

THURSDAY 1st DECEMBER 2011

Victoria's pace bowler James Pattinson made his Test debut for Australia, against New Zealand at the Gabba, Brisbane. His first appearance couldn't have gone much better – six wickets, including five in the second innings – and a man of the match award in his side's nine-wicket victory. The significance of the selection meant that for the first time in more than a century, two brothers had represented different countries in Tests. Nottinghamshire's Darren Pattinson had played for England against South Africa at Headingley in 2008. In the late 19th century Frank Hearne played Test cricket for England and later, having settled in South Africa, for that country against England. In the Cape Town Test of 1892 Frank played for South Africa, while his two brothers, George and Alec, were in the opposition XI.

THURSDAY 1st DECEMBER 2011

Nottinghamshire announced the signing of Leicestershire batsman James Taylor. Born in Nottingham, in January 1990, Taylor joined on a three-year deal, having played once for England, a one-day international against Ireland in August 2011.

FRIDAY 2nd DECEMBER 1932

Harold Larwood bowled the first delivery of what became known as the Bodyline series. The Nottinghamshire fast bowler returned 5-96 and 5-28 as England eased to a comfortable victory in the opening Test at Sydney, although Australia were without their best batsman, Donald Bradman, who was ill.

THURSDAY 3rd DECEMBER 1953

In a five-day representative match at Bombay, Nottinghamshire batsman Reg Simpson scored 121 for a Commonwealth XI against India. During the 16-match tour, Simpson played in nine fixtures and topped the batting averages with 750 runs at 53.57.

TUESDAY 3rd DECEMBER 1991

Willis Walker played his first match for Nottinghamshire in 1913 and his final one in August 1937 aged 44. In between, the right-handed batsman scored 18,242 runs from 405 matches. Averaging 32.45 on each visit to the wicket, he was amongst the ten highest aggregate all-time run-scorers for the county when he retired. The largest of his 31 centuries was the unbeaten 165 he posted in 1930, against Middlesex at Lord's, and he was close to another century at the time of his death in Keighley, Yorkshire, as he was 99-years-old.

SATURDAY 4th DECEMBER 1858

Dual international sportsman William "Billy" Gunn was born at St Ann's, Nottingham. As an amateur footballer he represented Nottingham Forest and Notts County and won two full England caps. As a 6'2" tall, right-handed batsman he scored 18,295 runs for Nottinghamshire between 1880 and 1904, averaging 34.06. He scored 48 centuries during his first-class career, with six of them converted into double-hundreds. Gunn played 11 Tests for England, with his final one the inaugural Test at Trent Bridge in 1899. Both of his nephews, John Gunn and George Gunn, would also go on to play for their country in later years. He died of cancer in 1921, aged 62.

FRIDAY 5th DECEMBER 1873

Born in 1814, John Buttery was an opening batsman and medium-pace bowler, who got his opportunity with the county side with a debut against MCC in 1843 but he only played three more times for Notts. Buttery later became an umpire and stood in first-class matches – but after being unable to shake off a severe cold he died on this day at his home in Nottingham.

FRIDAY 6th DECEMBER 1907

Charles Bowmar Harris formed one half of Nottinghamshire's strongest opening partnership in the pre-Second World War years. Alongside Walter Keeton, he helped add 2,269 runs in 44 stands at an average of 52. Born in Underwood, Harris first played for Nottinghamshire in 1928 but didn't hold down a regular place for another three seasons. In 1932 he topped 1,000 runs for the first time but didn't make a century – but remedied that a year later, hitting 234 against Middlesex. He lost six years of his career to the war but still scored 18,823 runs for Notts, as well as taking 196 wickets, with a best of 8-80. Renowned for his good humour and love of a prank, he scored his second career double-hundred at Trent Bridge against Hampshire in 1950, 239 not out.

WEDNESDAY 6th DECEMBER 1967

Right-arm fast-medium bowler Mark Nicholas Bowen joined Nottinghamshire in 1996 after beginning his career with Northamptonshire. Born in Redcar, Yorkshire, he spent five years at Trent Bridge, picking up 153 wickets in 54 first-class matches and 56 in 48 List A games. With a BSc in chemical engineering behind him, he left the game aged 32 to join British Nuclear Fuels at Sellafield.

FRIDAY 6th DECEMBER 1968

After concluding his maiden season of county cricket with Nottinghamshire, Garfield Sobers flew to Australia to captain the West Indies in a five-match series. During the opening Test, at Brisbane, Sobers produced the best figures of his international career, taking 6-73 in the second innings to inspire his side to victory.

SUNDAY 7th DECEMBER 1856

Born in Calverton, Nottinghamshire, Wilfred Flowers became the first Notts player to complete the cricketing double of 1,000 runs and 100 wickets in a season. That same year, 1883, saw him amass 1,144 runs, the most productive campaign of his career. He twice toured Australia, making his England debut at Adelaide in 1884, the first of his eight Test appearances. A right-handed batsman and off-break bowler, Flowers played 281 matches for Notts, scoring 8,252 runs and taking 714 wickets.

FRANKLYN STEPHENSON DID THE DOUBLE FOR NOTTS IN 1988

TUESDAY 7th DECEMBER 1999

Paul Franks made 11 appearances for England A over a six-year period, touring South Africa, Bangladesh, New Zealand, the West Indies and Sri Lanka. His best bowling performance came against Central Districts at Palmerston North, New Zealand, where his second-innings figures of 5-26, from 19.2 overs, helped secure a 95-run victory.

TUESDAY 8th DECEMBER 1885

Right-arm fast-medium bowler Cecil Cooper Clifton was born in Eastwood, Nottinghamshire, and made his debut for the county side in 1908. In 24 first-class appearances he took 50 wickets, at 26.68, with a best of 4-25 at Trent Bridge against Lancashire. His batting was limited, with a top score of only 22 and an average of just above five. Clifton then spent two years in the Lancashire League, as well as making 31 appearances for Cheshire in the Minor Counties Championship before dying in Liverpool in 1930, aged 44.

SUNDAY 9th DECEMBER 1866

Although John Sharpe was born in Ruddington, Nottinghamshire, he couldn't force his early way into the Nottinghamshire side and joined Surrey as a fast-medium bowler. In his first game for them in 1899, he returned extraordinary figures of 21.1-18-5-5 against Oxford University. He played three Tests for England before joining Nottinghamshire in 1894 but he only made five appearances, taking a modest ten wickets. Having lost an eye earlier in his life, he was limited as a batsman and in the field, and aged 28 he called time on his cricketing career. John's father, Samuel Sharpe, made two appearances for Notts in 1868.

MONDAY 10th DECEMBER 2007

Although not having yet played for Nottinghamshire, Stuart Broad had already completed his move from Leicestershire ahead of his Test match debut for England. Opening the bowling with Ryan Sidebottom, against Sri Lanka in Colombo, it was therefore the first instance of the county providing both new-ball bowlers in a Test since Larwood and Voce 74 years earlier. Broad's first wicket at this level was Chaminder Vaas, caught by Ian Bell. In the drawn contest, the debutant's first Test analysis was 36-5-95-1.

MONDAY 11th DECEMBER 1967

Slow left-arm spinner Richard David Stemp was born in Erdington, Warwickshire, and appeared for Worcestershire and Yorkshire ahead of his Nottinghamshire debut in 1999. His 29 first-class matches for the county delivered 65 wickets, with a best of 5-123. A lower-order right-handed batsman, he posted a career-best 66 against Hampshire at The Rose Bowl in 2001. His 48 List A matches for Notts yielded 48 wickets at an average of 33.04.

TUESDAY 11th DECEMBER 1979

In a first-class career which spanned 22 years, Derek Randall only took 13 wickets. It was something of a surprise, therefore, when England skipper Mike Brearley lobbed the ball to the Nottinghamshire man in an ODI against Australia at Sydney. To be fair to the captain, his side were well on top with Australia needing 74 from just three overs and their last pair at the crease. Victoria's Trevor Laughlin hit the first delivery for two runs before spooning the next in the air for Graham Gooch to catch. Randall's complete ODI analysis remained 0.2-0-2-1.

THURSDAY 11th DECEMBER 2008

It's probably fair to say that Graeme Swann's introduction into Test cricket couldn't have got off to a better start. Making his debut against India in Chennai, the off-spinner was brought on to bowl the 14th over of the innings. With just his third delivery he had the left-handed Gautam Gambhir out lbw – and with the sixth ball, he did the same to right-handed Rahul Dravid, becoming only the second England bowler, after Richard Johnson, to take two wickets in his maiden Test over.

FRIDAY 12th DECEMBER 1884

One of five Nottinghamshire players in the England side, Billy Barnes' only Test century came against Australia at Adelaide when he made 134. William Scotton, captain Arthur Shrewsbury and debutants Wilf Flowers and William Attewell also competed in a match won by the tourists inside four days. Apart from Attewell, the others occupied the top four positions in the order in the second innings, showing the strength of Nottinghamshire's batting at the time.

FRIDAY 13th DECEMBER 1901

John Gunn played six Tests for England, the first five coming in Australia on the 1901/02 tour. His debut was at the Sydney Cricket Ground, where he made 21 as England triumphed by an innings. He also bowled five overs without claiming a wicket.

FRIDAY 13th DECEMBER 1907

George Gunn's Test debut came against Australia at Sydney, six years to the day after his elder brother John's. He made 119 in the first innings and 74 in the second. Another Nottinghamshire debutant, Joe Hardstaff senior, scored 12 and 63 in the first of his five Tests, although the match was won by the Australians.

FRIDAY 13th DECEMBER 1963

Duncan John Richardson Martindale was born in Harrogate, Yorkshire. Although he made 55 first-class appearances for Nottinghamshire, he is perhaps best remembered for being called in for his one-day debut in the 1985 NatWest Trophy final, then being at the non-striker's end as Derek Randall just failed in his bid to score 18 off the final over. Martindale scored four centuries for Notts in the longer format of the game, with a best of 138 against Cambridge University in 1990.

THURSDAY 14th DECEMBER 1967

Despite several counties being in the running to secure his services, Nottinghamshire were able to announce that Garfield Sobers had signed for them – and been appointed captain – ahead of the 1968 domestic season. Although further details were undisclosed at the time, *Wisden* 1968 reported that Sobers' contract would run for an initial three years and be worth £7,000 per annum and include an apartment and a car.

SATURDAY 15th DECEMBER 1984

In his second appearance for England, Tim Robinson scored the first of his four Test centuries. Playing against India the Nottinghamshire opener advanced to 160 before being caught by Sunil Gavaskar, from the bowling of Kapil Dev. His innings had lasted for 508 minutes, during which time he faced 390 deliveries, 17 of which were hit for boundaries.

THURSDAY 16th DECEMBER 1948

Reg Simpson made a disappointing entrance into Test cricket. The Nottinghamshire batsman made scores of 5 and 0 on his first appearance for England, against South Africa at Kingsmead in Durban.

SUNDAY 16th DECEMBER 2007

Playing in the inaugural Indian Cricket League, Chris Read was a member of the winning side. In the final of the Twenty20 tournament, Read's Chennai Superstars defeated Chandigarh Lions by 12 runs at Panchkula, with the Nottinghamshire wicketkeeper scoring 21. In the three-week, six-team tournament, Read played seven games and scored 140 runs, with a best of 37.

THURSDAY 17th DECEMBER 2009

Graeme Swann's first Test on South African soil turned into an individual triumph for the off-spinning all-rounder. In the home side's first-innings 418, Swann was given a hefty workload, getting through 45.2 overs for figures of 5-110. Coming to the crease at 221-7 he then hit a typically robust 85, from just 81 deliveries, with ten fours and two sixes. South Africa had the better of the overall contest, which ended in a draw, but the man of the match spoils at Centurion Park had already been secured by the Nottinghamshire man.

MONDAY 18th DECEMBER 1922

Born in 1839 in West Leake, Nottinghamshire, Augustus Bateman was the youngest of a family of cricketing siblings. John Bateman played for Derbyshire and Cambridge University and Edward Bateman played once for Notts in 1855. After moving to St John's, Cambridge, Augustus gained selection against Oxford in three consecutive seasons, earning plaudits for his wicketkeeping. In 1862 he made his only appearance for Nottinghamshire, scoring 63 against Surrey at Trent Bridge. Not only was his innings the top score in the match, which Notts won, but he was dismissed in circumstances that wouldn't be permitted today as a Surrey fieldsman, Billy Caffyn, ran amongst the spectators to take an outstanding catch. In that era the ball had to be hit out of the ground to count as a six, there being no boundary rope or line. Augustus was 83 when he died in Nottingham.

THURSDAY 19th DECEMBER 1935

Christopher Grant was born in Lincoln and was a prolific run-scorer for the Newark club for many years, as well as featuring regularly for the Nottinghamshire second XI. His first-team experience was limited to three matches in 1968, against Derbyshire, Sussex and the Australian tourists. Perhaps uniquely, although the fixtures were played over a short space of time, he appeared under three different captains, Deryck Murray, Garfield Sobers and Brian Bolus. He also played in one Gillette Cup tie, away at New Road against Worcestershire.

THURSDAY 20th DECEMBER 2007

John Cook, born in June 1946, was a serving police officer when he made a handful of appearances for Nottinghamshire in the mid-1970s. An off-spinner, with an affiliation to Retford CC and the successful county police side, he played in two championship matches and ten one-day fixtures, with a best return of 4-19 against Surrey in 1974. Dogged by ill health for a number of years, he died in a Nottingham hospital at the age of 61.

MONDAY 21st DECEMBER 1914

Arthur Owen Jones, who played for Nottinghamshire between 1892 and 1914, was just 42 years of age when he died of tuberculosis on this day in Dunstable, Bedfordshire. Jones played in 12 Test matches for England and captained them on two occasions. A right-handed opening batsman, he played in 397 first-class matches for Notts, scoring 20,244 runs at an average of 33.02. In 1903 his unbeaten score of 296, against Gloucestershire at Trent Bridge, was then the highest score recorded by a Nottinghamshire batsman. Jones' right-arm leg-breaks and googlies also claimed 294 wickets for his county.

MONDAY 22nd DECEMBER 1958

Christopher Colin Curzon was born in Nottingham, the younger brother of John Curzon, who played once for Notts in 1978. Chris made his debut in the same season (though didn't play in the same match as his brother) and went on to make 17 first-class appearances, as well as 11 List A outings. A right-handed batsman and wicketkeeper, he was unable to score above 45 in any of his county appearances.

MONDAY 22nd DECEMBER 1947

Born in Rajkot, Gujarat, India, Dilip Rasiklal Doshi made his Nottinghamshire debut against the 1973 West Indian tourists, after playing just two times for the second XI. Over the next couple of years he was restricted to non-championship fixtures but Doshi went on to play in a total of 44 matches for the county after qualifying, taking 157 wickets at 29.22. The bespectacled slow left-arm spinner left Notts at the end of the 1978 season and a year later was making the first of his 33 Test appearances for India.

SATURDAY 23rd DECEMBER 1922

The first of Arthur Carr's 11 Test appearances for England came against South Africa at the Old Wanderers ground in Johannesburg. The Nottinghamshire skipper made 27 in each innings of his debut match, the first of them coming on an opening day which saw 18 wickets fall. Both sides then enjoyed two full rest days before the contest resumed on Boxing Day, with the home side going on to claim victory by 168 runs.

MONDAY 24th DECEMBER 1798

The man who is generally acknowledged to have been at the forefront of cricket in his home county was born in Nottingham. After marrying Mary Chapman, the widowed landlady of the Trent Bridge Inn, William Clarke cleared up the old meadow at the back of the inn, rendering it fit for the county side to move into, and from July 1840 it became the home of Nottinghamshire County Cricket Club.

THURSDAY 25th DECEMBER 1862

Arthur Pike was born in Keyworth and also died there 44 years later. His role within the Nottinghamshire side was usually as a lower-order batsman who kept wicket. In 44 matches for the county he scored just over 1,100 runs with a top score of 66 and took 99 catches, with 28 stumpings. In 1901, two years after his final appearance, he turned out once for MCC, at Lord's against Kent. Pike then stood as an umpire in 85 first-class fixtures up until his death on 15th November 1907.

WEDNESDAY 25th DECEMBER 1963

Ashley Anthony Metcalfe spent two years at Nottinghamshire after playing the bulk of his career with his native Yorkshire. Born in Horsforth, near Leeds, he scored over 10,000 runs before leaving Headingley, at an average of 35.11. Whilst at Trent Bridge he was able to add to his 25 centuries with a score of 128, against Glamorgan at Worksop in 1996.

FRIDAY 26th DECEMBER 1873

Sutton-in-Ashfield was the birthplace of the man who became Nottinghamshire's record wicket-taker. Thomas Wass was tall and solidly built and was quick through the air with a dangerous leg-cutter. He made his debut in 1896 but his figures remained modest until 1900 when he spearheaded the bowling alongside John Gunn. That season he took 108 wickets at just over 18 each, the first of ten seasons in which he broke the century barrier. His best year was 1907, when he dismissed 163 victims as Nottinghamshire enjoyed an undefeated title-winning campaign. That same year Wass was chosen in a pre-match 13 for the first Test against South Africa at Lord's but was omitted from the starting XI and not called upon again. Nicknamed "Topsy", he played 308 matches for Notts, taking 1,653 wickets at an average of 20.33. His best return was 9-67 against Derbyshire at Blackwell. His only innings of note also came against Derbyshire but he was dropped four times in his 56. He was 79 when he died, also at Sutton-in-Ashfield.

FRIDAY 27th DECEMBER 1957

Kevin Edwin Cooper was born in Sutton-in-Ashfield and made his Nottinghamshire debut in 1976, taking four wickets in each innings against Cambridge University. The tall, right-arm seamer established himself as a key component of the Notts attack as he clocked up 272 first-class appearances over 17 seasons, which produced a harvest of 711 victims and 16th spot in the all-time list of the county's wicket-takers. His best figures were 8-44 against Middlesex at Lord's in 1984. Four years later Cooper topped 100 wickets for the season, with 101 – his best seasonal return. In 250 List A matches, which included Lord's finals in 1982, 1985 and 1989, he claimed another 244 wickets at 31.86.

SATURDAY 28th DECEMBER 1872

Arthur Wilkinson played 19 first-class matches for Nottinghamshire, scoring 293 runs and taking 33 wickets. Born in Nottingham, he had played for Notts Colts and in the Lancashire League before making his county debut, at Trent Bridge against Somerset in 1894. Wilkinson made one half-century and claimed one five-wicket haul before his first-class career ended just one year after it had begun.

WEDNESDAY 29th DECEMBER 2010

England completed an innings victory over Australia in Melbourne, going 2-1 up in the five-match series and guaranteeing that the Ashes would be retained (England later won the last Test for a 3-1 series win). The post-match celebrations included Nottinghamshire's Graeme Swann, who had taken 2-59 from 27 overs on the final day of the match, leading his team-mates and thousands of jubilant England supporters in a choreographed rendition of the "Sprinkler" dance.

SUNDAY 30th DECEMBER 1951

Although the match was drawn, Cyril Poole enjoyed a fine individual match on his Test debut for England, against India at Eden Gardens, Calcutta. The Nottinghamshire batsman scored 55 in his first innings and an unbeaten 69 second time around. He appeared in the next two Test matches, at Kanpur and Madras, but wasn't selected again.

SATURDAY 30th DECEMBER 1961

Nottinghamshire's wicketkeeper Geoff Millman made his England debut against India at Eden Gardens, Calcutta. Although he missed out with the bat, registering scores of 0 and 4, he kept tidily throughout and claimed five dismissals in a match that the home side won by 187 runs.

SATURDAY 31st DECEMBER 1881

England gave New Year's Eve Test debuts to two Nottinghamshire batsmen in the opening match of their series against Australia at the MCG. William Scotton was run out for 21 in the first innings but made an unbeaten 50 in the second, whilst Arthur Shrewsbury scored 11 and 16. Two county colleagues, England captain Alfred Shaw and John Selby, were also included in the drawn fixture.